The Magical Girl's Self-Care Coloring Book

Jacque Aye
Venus Bambisa

COLOR YOUR WORLD AND EMBRACE YOUR INNER POWER

ULYSSES PRESS

Published by:
Ulysses Press
PO Box 3440
Berkeley, CA 94703
www.ulyssespress.com

ISBN: 978-1-64604-492-4

Printed in the United States by Sheridan Books Minnesota
2 4 6 8 10 9 7 5 3 1

INTRODUCTION

Hey, magical girl. You've been fighting those pesky monsters of the week with all you've got for so long. With your Magical Girl Gang by your side, and your furry familiar guiding your steps, you've managed to overcome much of the mayhem thrown your way by the Anxiety Monster, the Sultan of Self-Doubt, the Duke of Despair, and more. You've conquered the chaos, saved the city, and found love after fighting crime. But have you stopped to check in with yourself?

It's okay to slow down. Lay down your weapon, pick up a colored pencil, and relax.

The Magical Girl's Self-Care Coloring Book is here to serve as your self-care companion. When you're feeling weary from battle, or the chaos of the world becomes far too overwhelming, I want you to open this book, recite one of its magical mantras, and color your world with magic...and markers!

The magical beings in this book range from life-saving nurses to mystical mermaids and everything in between. And, of course, it wouldn't be a magical girl coloring book without whimsical weapons and adorable familiars. Sending all the thanks to Venus Bambisa, the amazing artist who brought the pages of this book to life.

Turn the page, and begin your self-care journey today.

—Jacque Aye

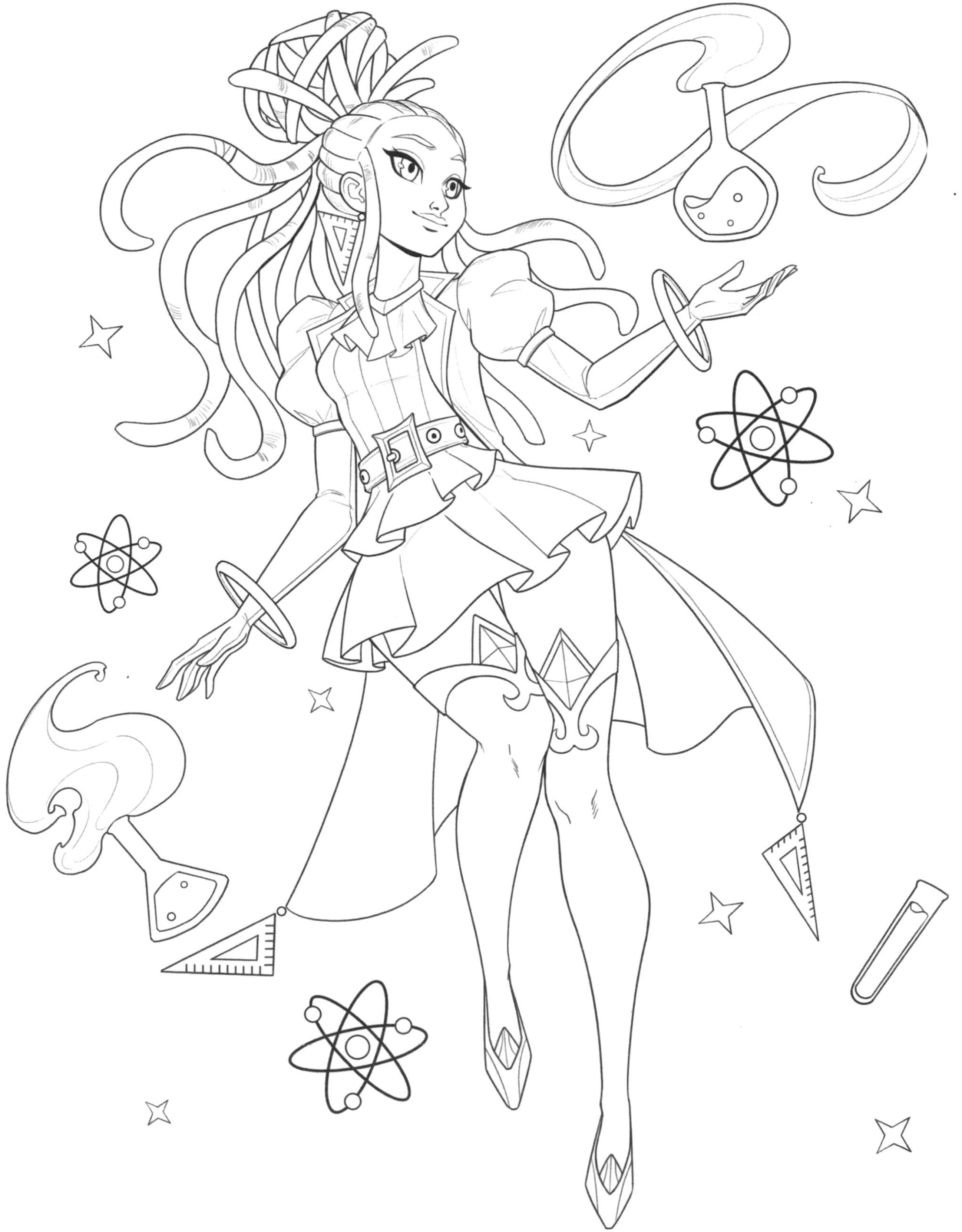

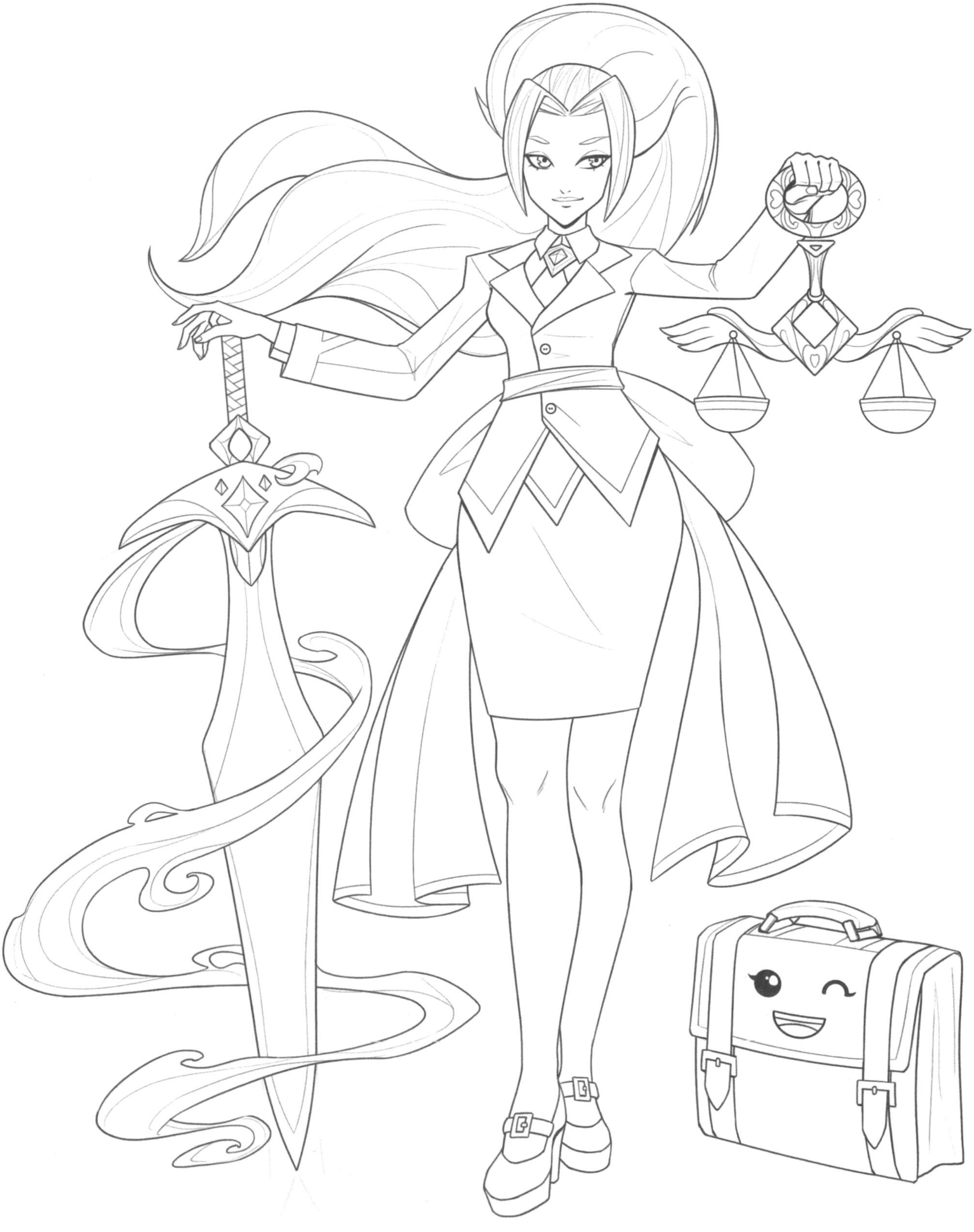

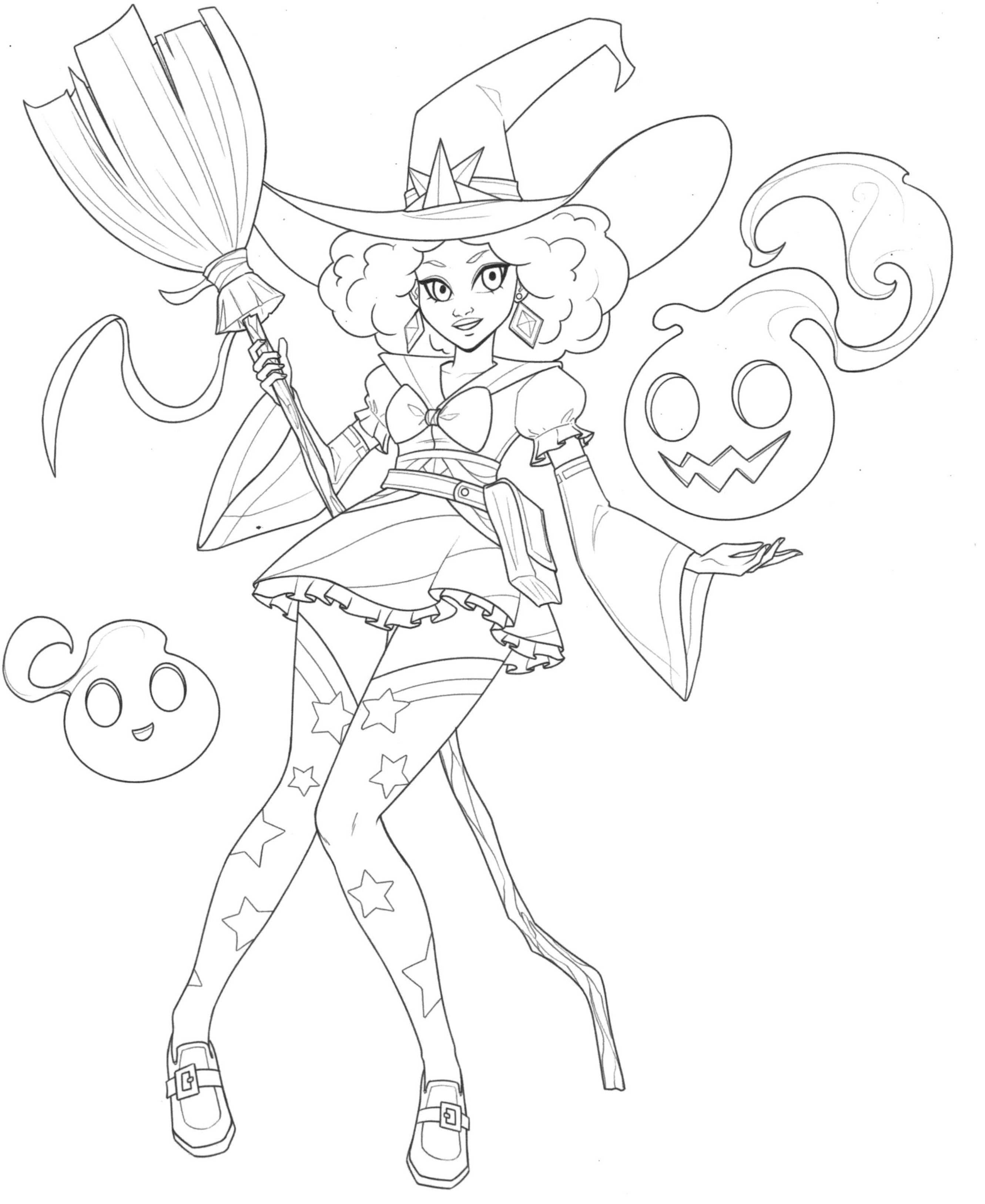

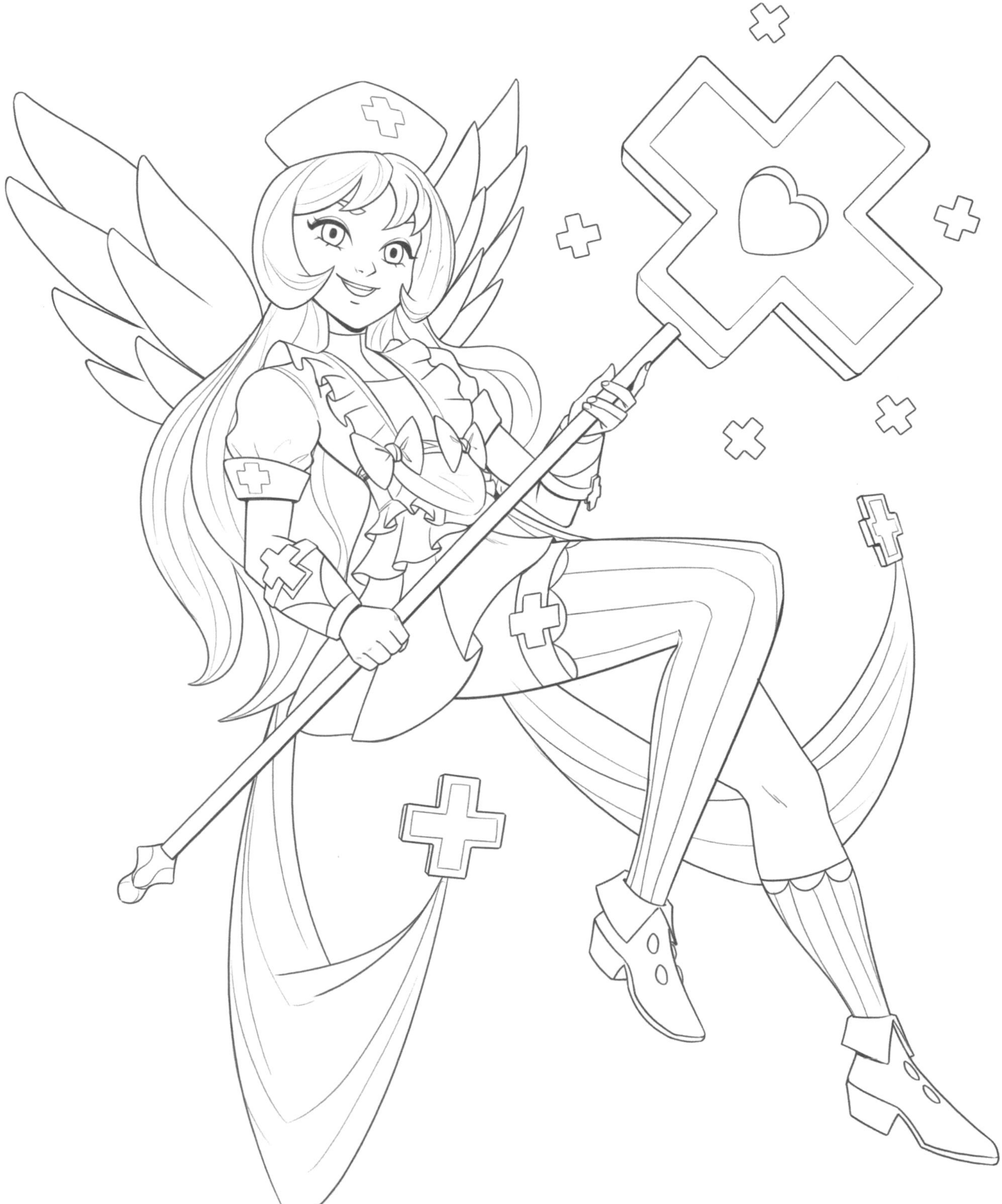

MAGICAL MANTRA FOR
HEARTBREAK

Many of us carry shields forged by wounds from past heartbreak. We never want to be heartbroken again, so we stash our hearts away in crystal cases behind towering walls. But don't let hurtful moments harden your soul. Learn from the past and create personal boundaries instead of an impenetrable fortress.

Repeat this:

I have learned so much about myself through my experiences. I reacted with the tools I had at the moment, and now I know what I will not allow in my magical space!

MAGICAL MANTRA FOR
FEELING SMALL

You don't need anyone's permission to take up space. Use your voice, stand your ground, and do what you love. Never shrink yourself to be more palatable to the tastes of other people.

Repeat this:

I deserve to take up space simply because I exist.

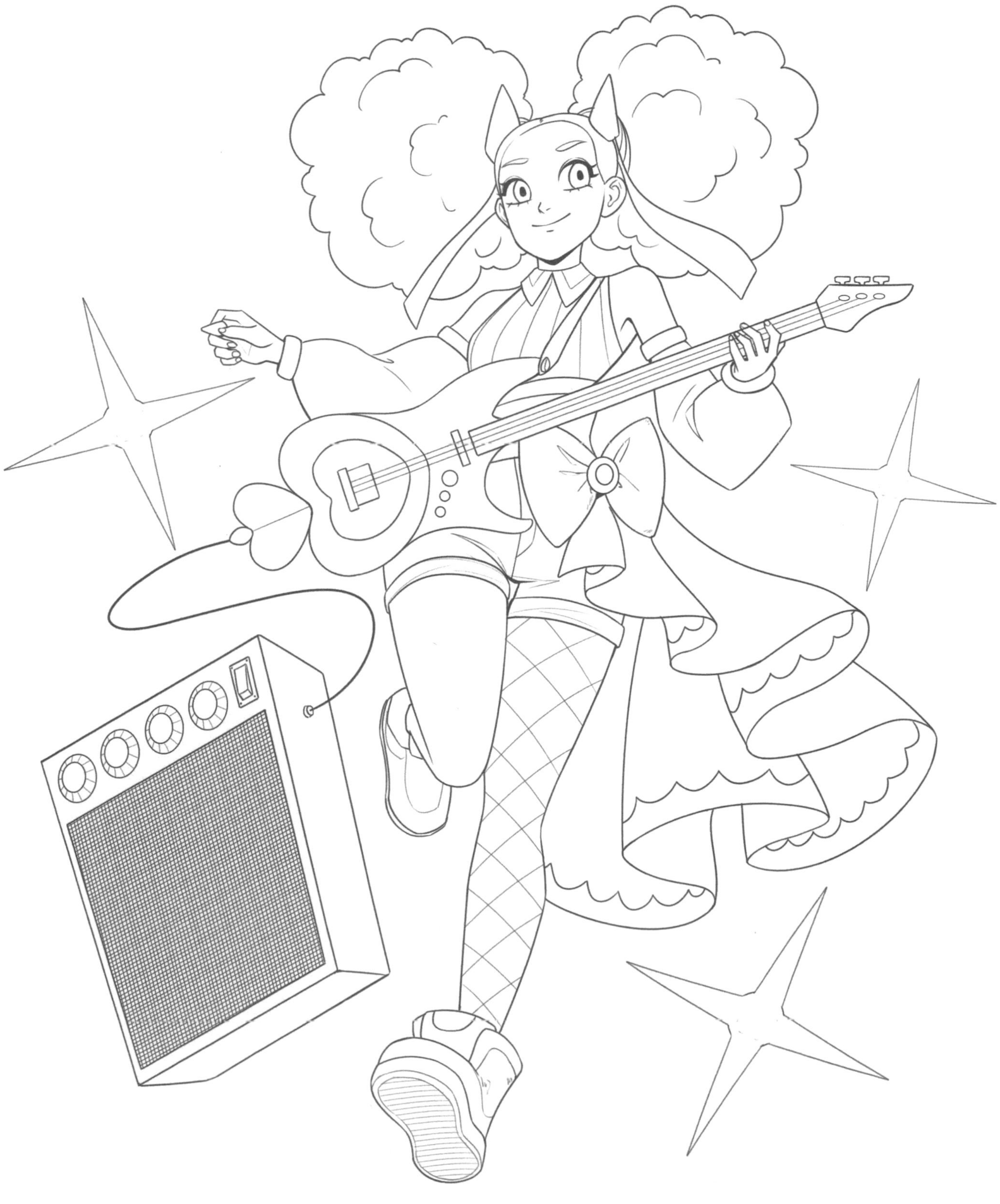

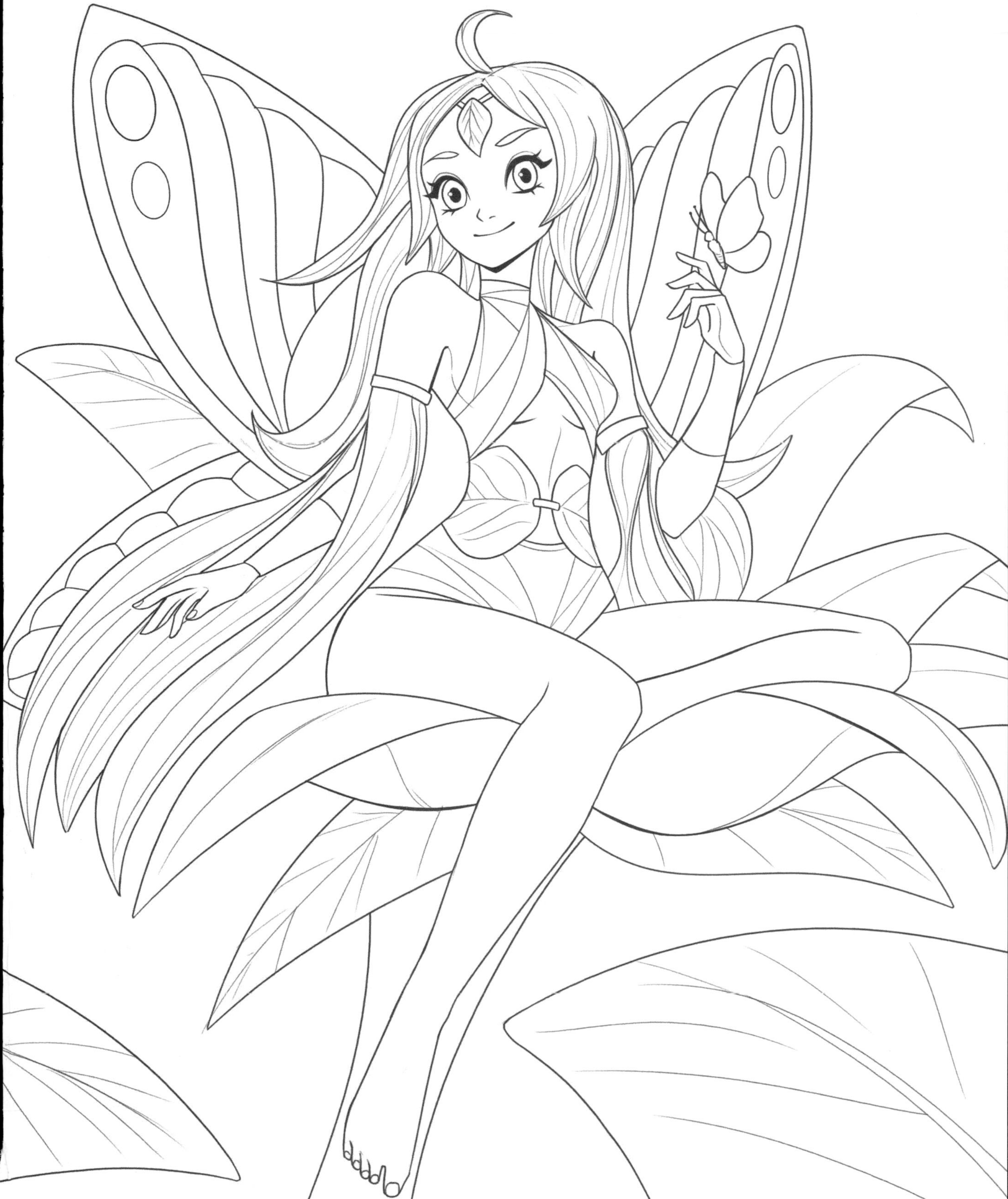

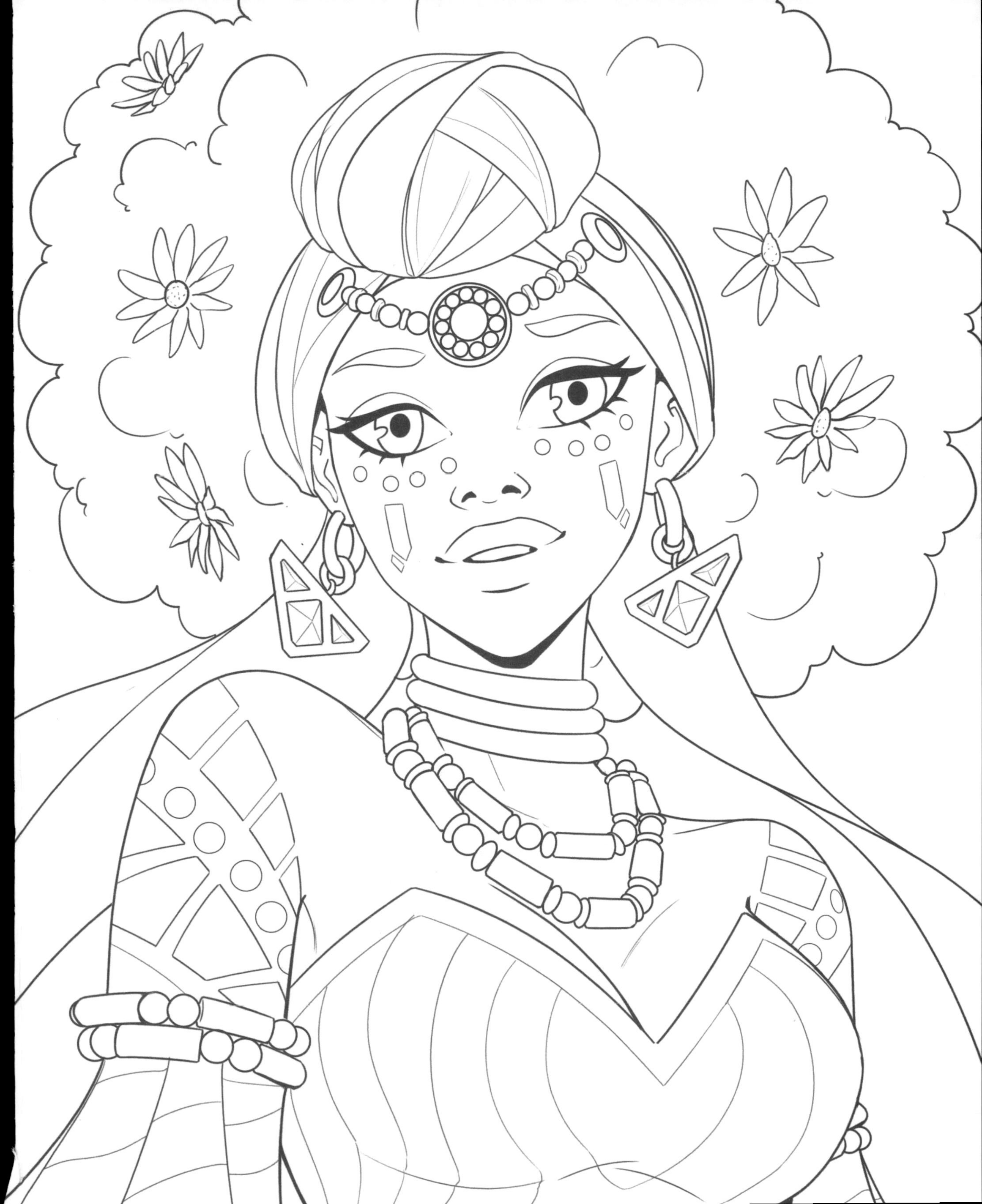

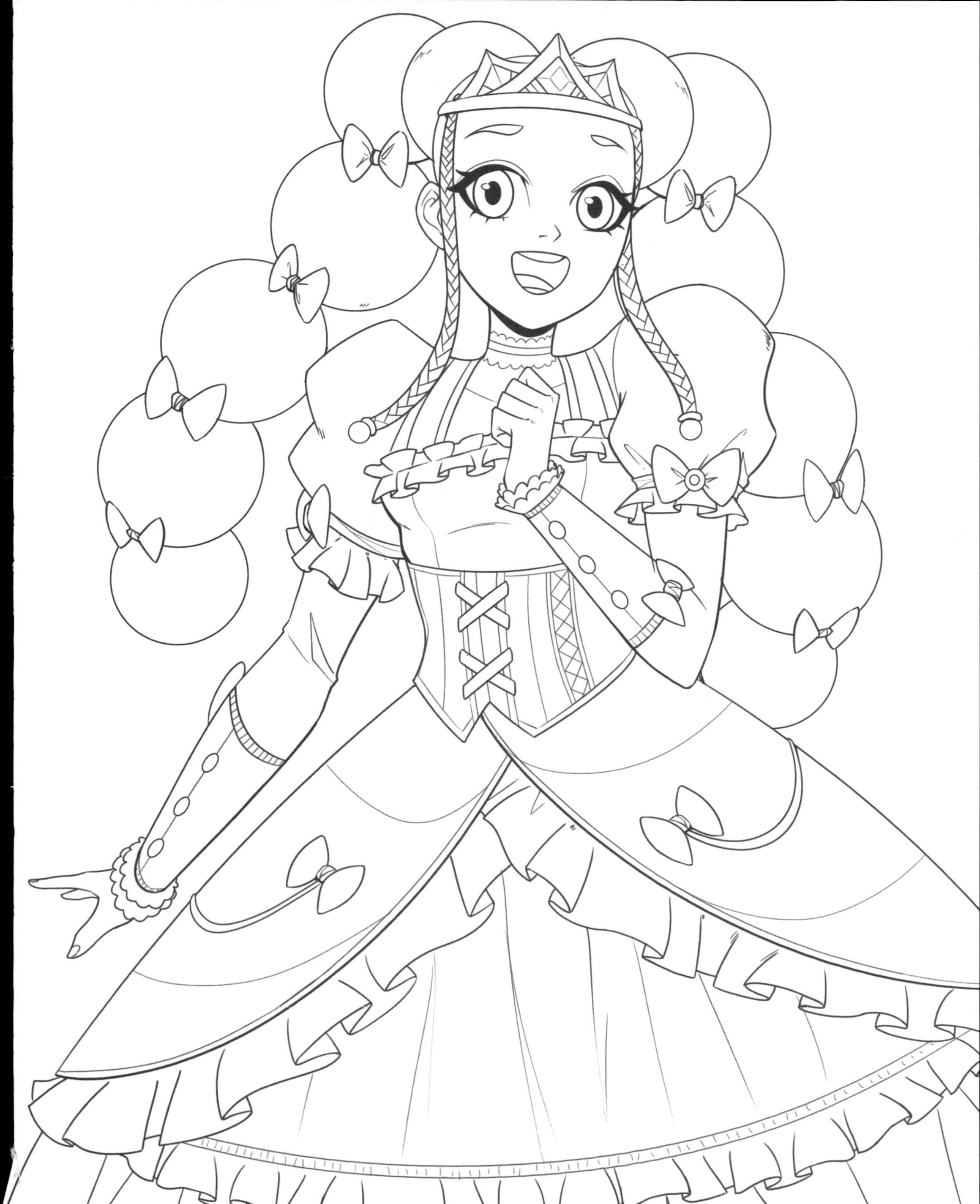

MAGICAL MANTRA FOR
FEELING DEFEATED

Your monster of the week's got nothing on you, magical girl! Some obstacles may be tougher than others, but know that you're powerful enough to overcome them. Rest up, recharge, and when you're ready, wield your scepter and charge back into battle!

Repeat this:

I give myself permission to try again without shame.

MAGICAL MANTRA FOR
FEELING MISUNDERSTOOD

Not everyone can comprehend the magic you possess, and that's okay! On a planet with eight billion people, you're bound to find someone who sees you. Open your heart to new experiences, be your authentic self, and be alright with doubters along the way. It will be worth it to find your Magical Girl Gang—trust me!

Repeat this:

I deserve to be seen.

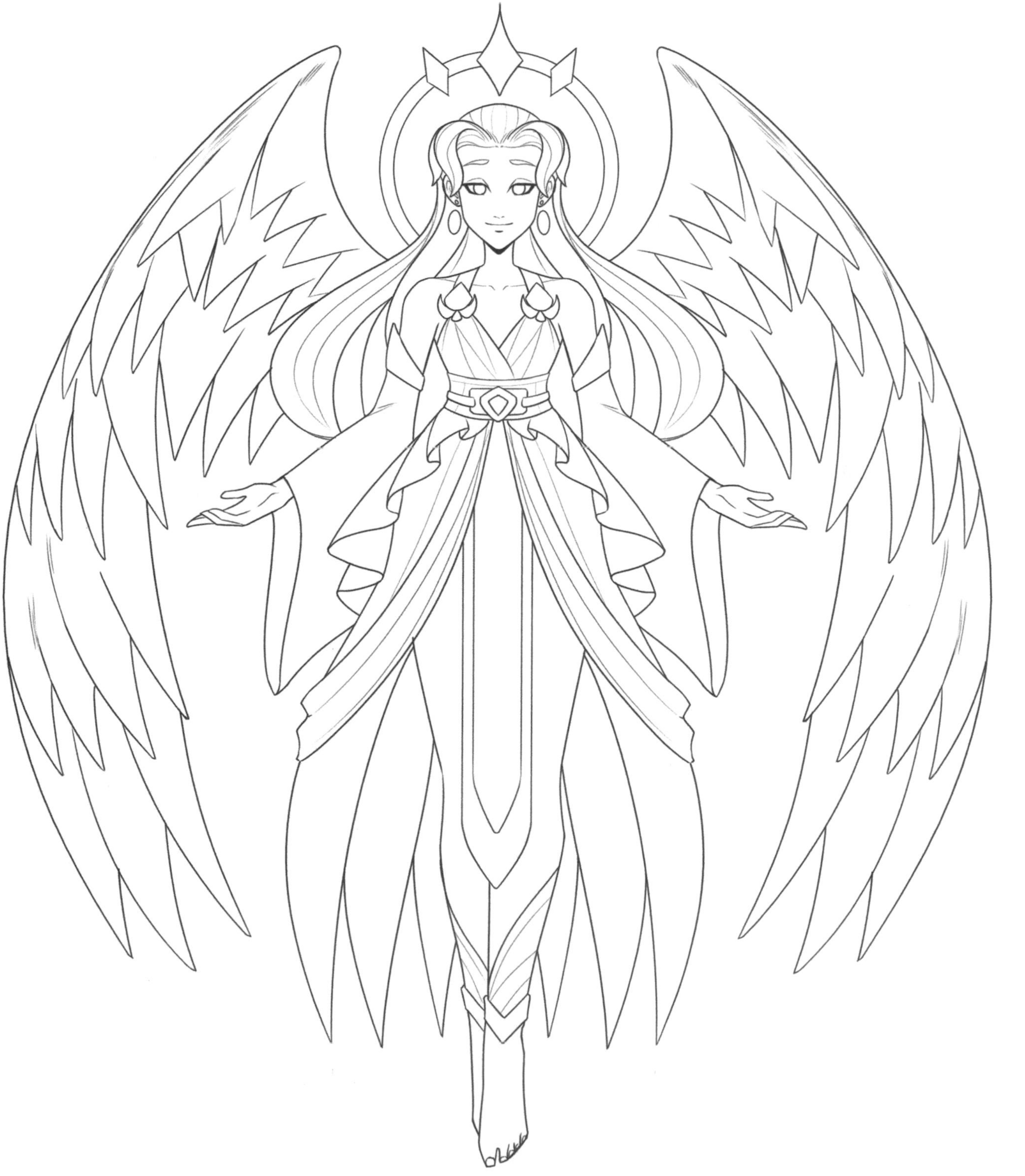

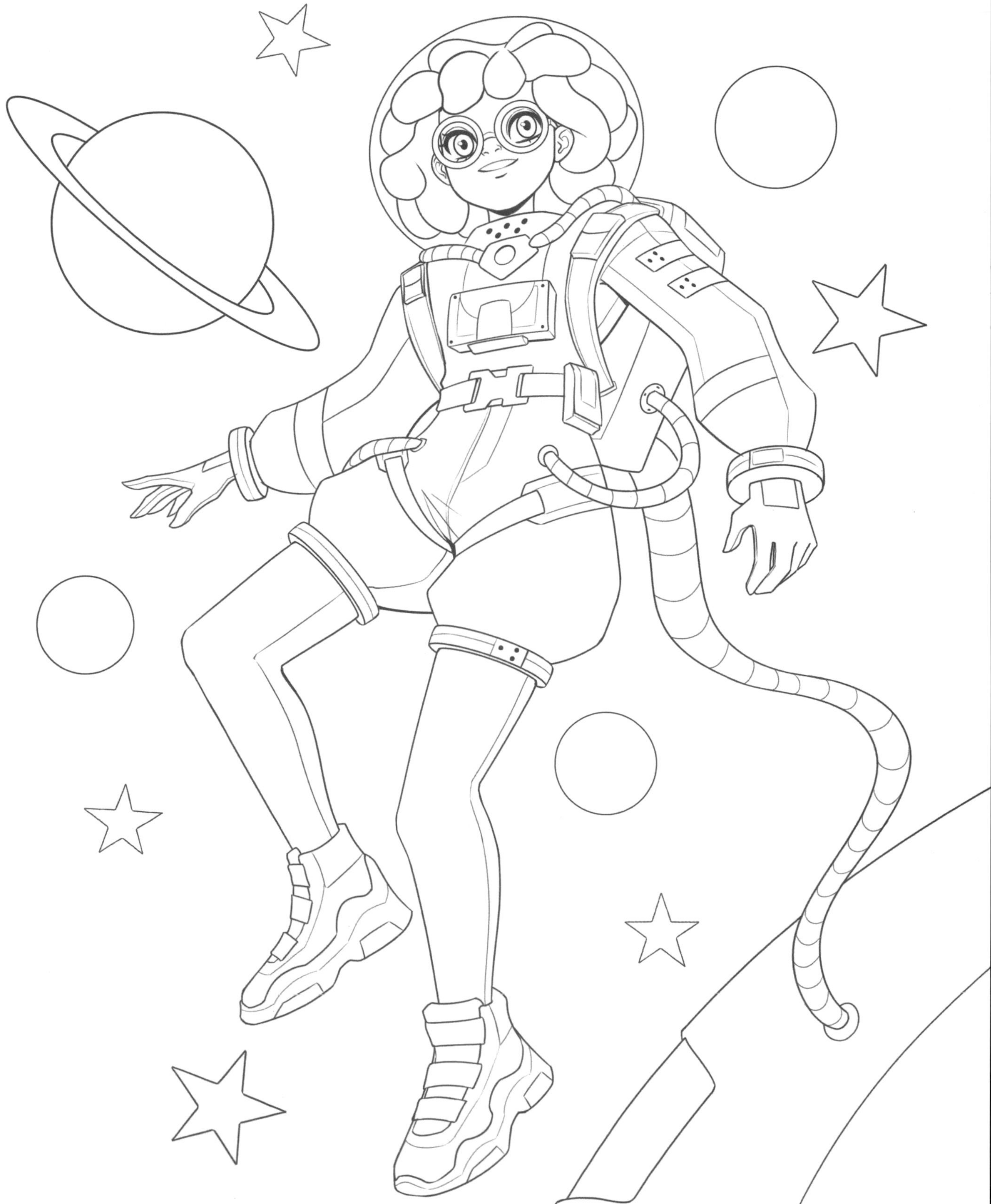

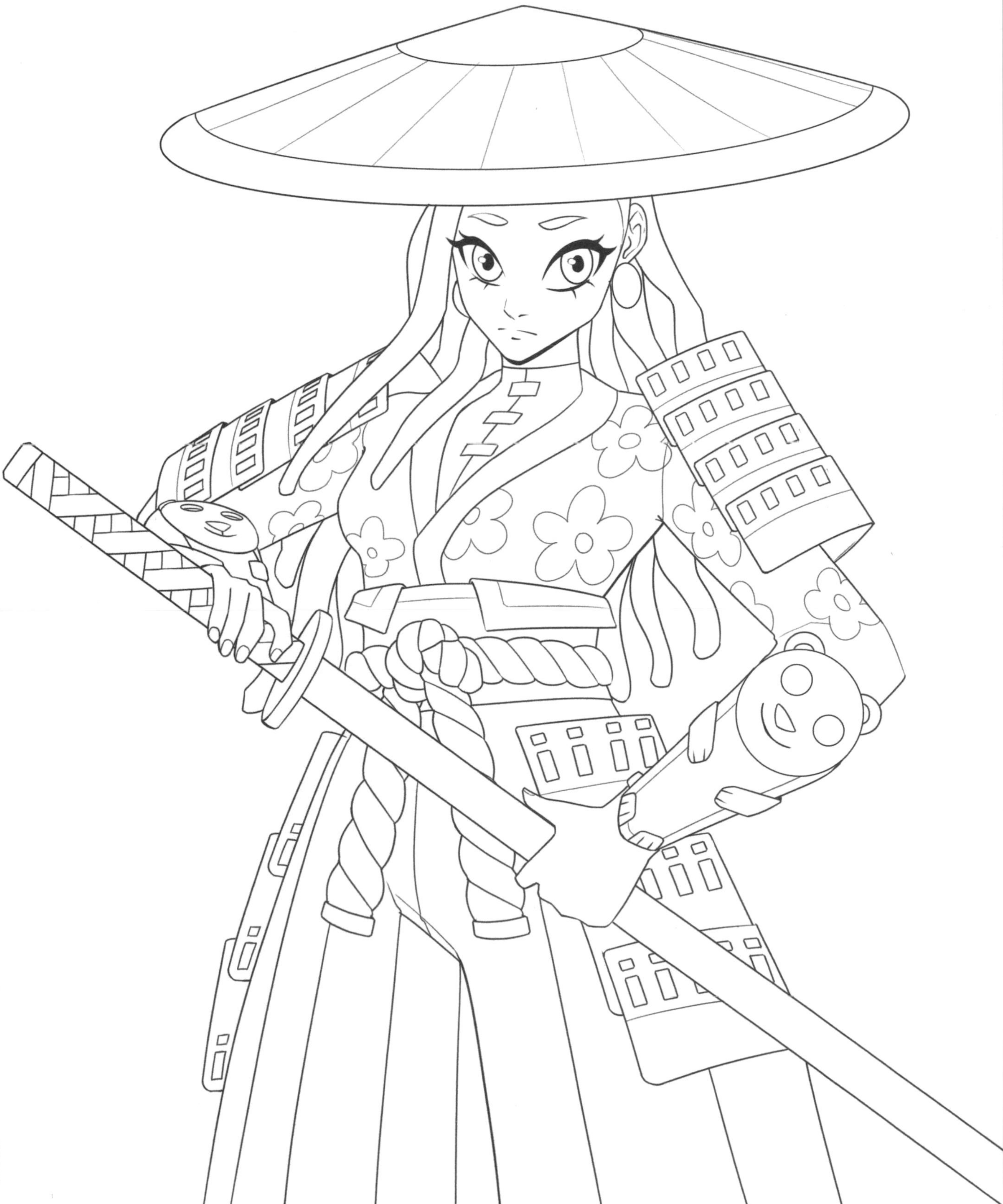

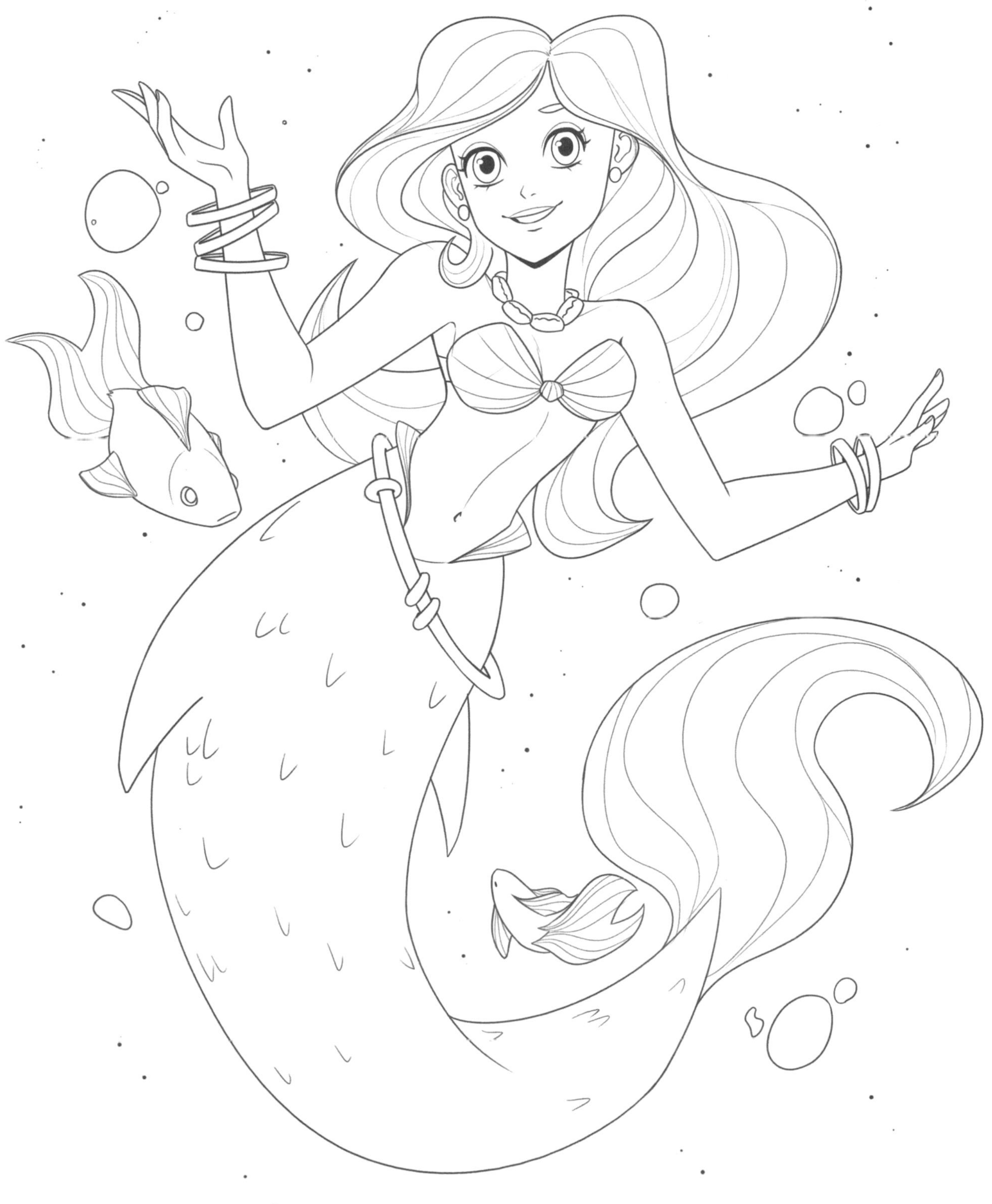

MAGICAL MANTRA FOR
REST

Whoa, magical girl. You've been fighting so hard for so long! Don't risk taking on too many battles and burning yourself out. It's okay to take breaks. It's okay to rest. Put away that scepter, lie down, and relax. You can't be the hero everyone needs every moment of the day.

Repeat this:

I give myself permission to rest.

MAGICAL MANTRA FOR
BOUNDARY SETTING

It's not mean, cruel, or selfish to set boundaries. In fact, it's one of the most powerful and magical things you can do as you move through the world. Boundaries teach people how to love you, how to care for you, and how to maintain the connection between you. Boundaries also keep people out, as purposefully crossing an established boundary is a clear sign of incompatibility.

A boundary is not an ultimatum or a towering wall. Rather, it's a cutely decorated door leading into a cozy cottage, where the community you build can safely sit and have tea in the afternoon.

Repeat this:

I'm not selfish for setting boundaries. I'm creating an environment where I feel safe with the people around me.

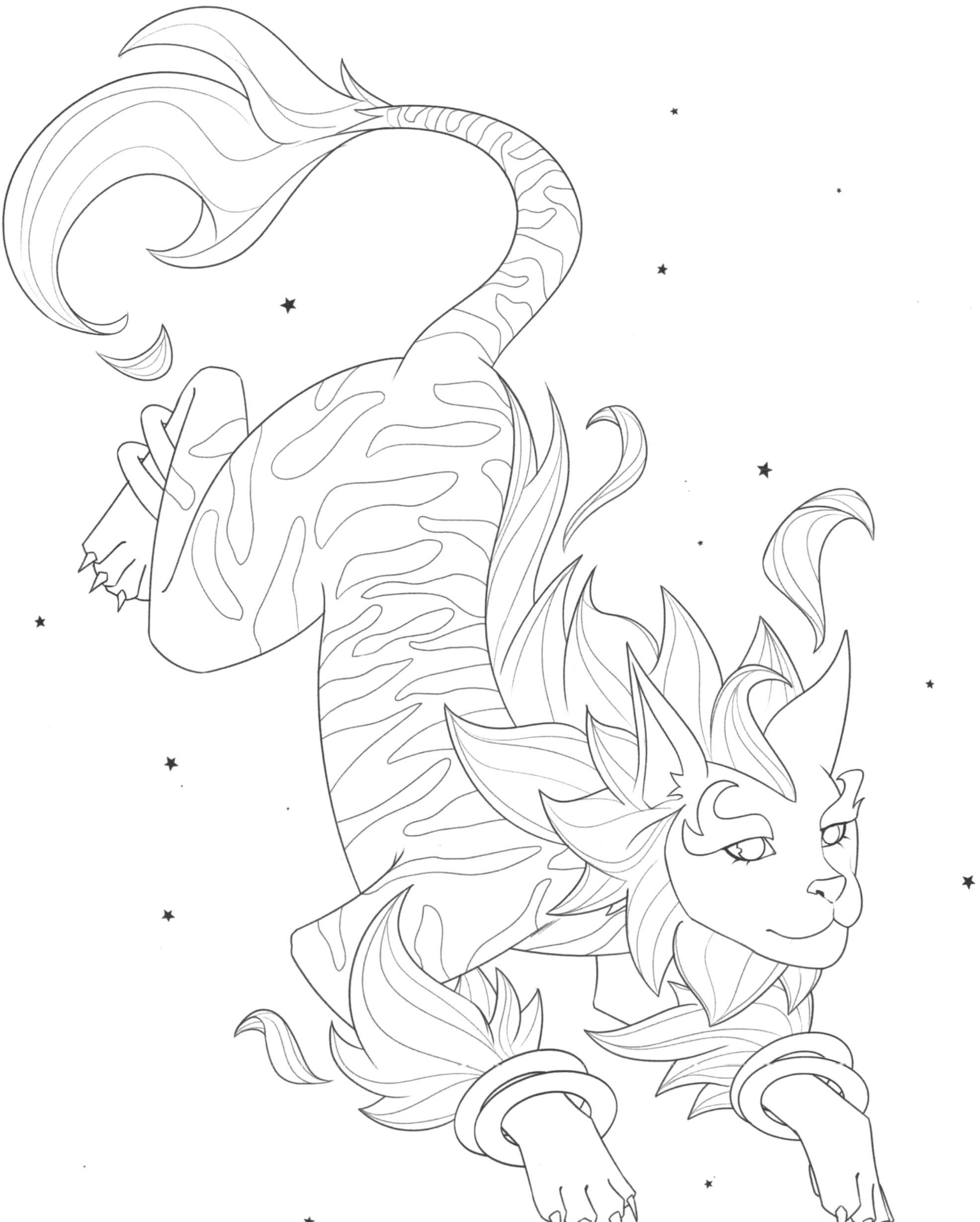

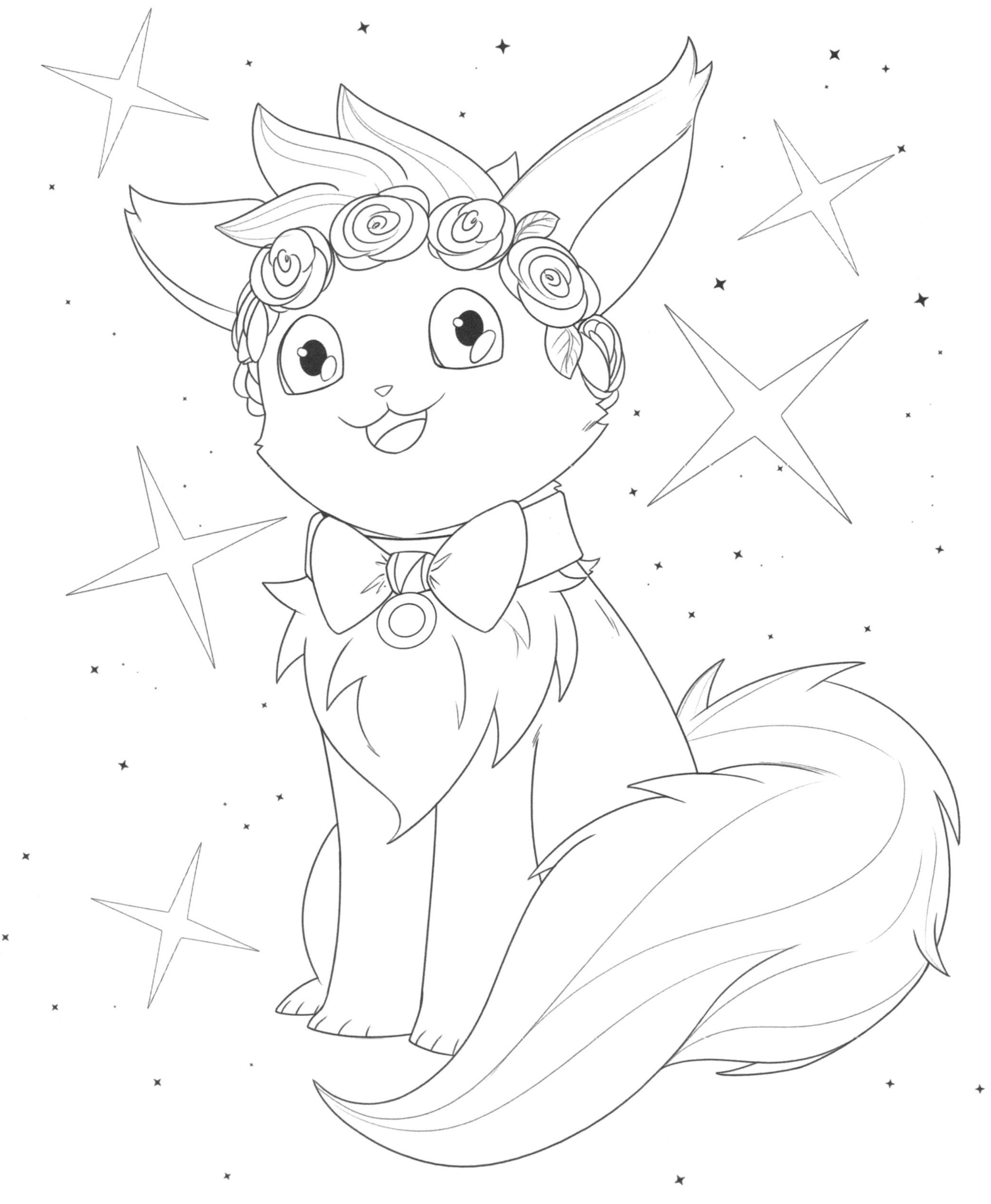

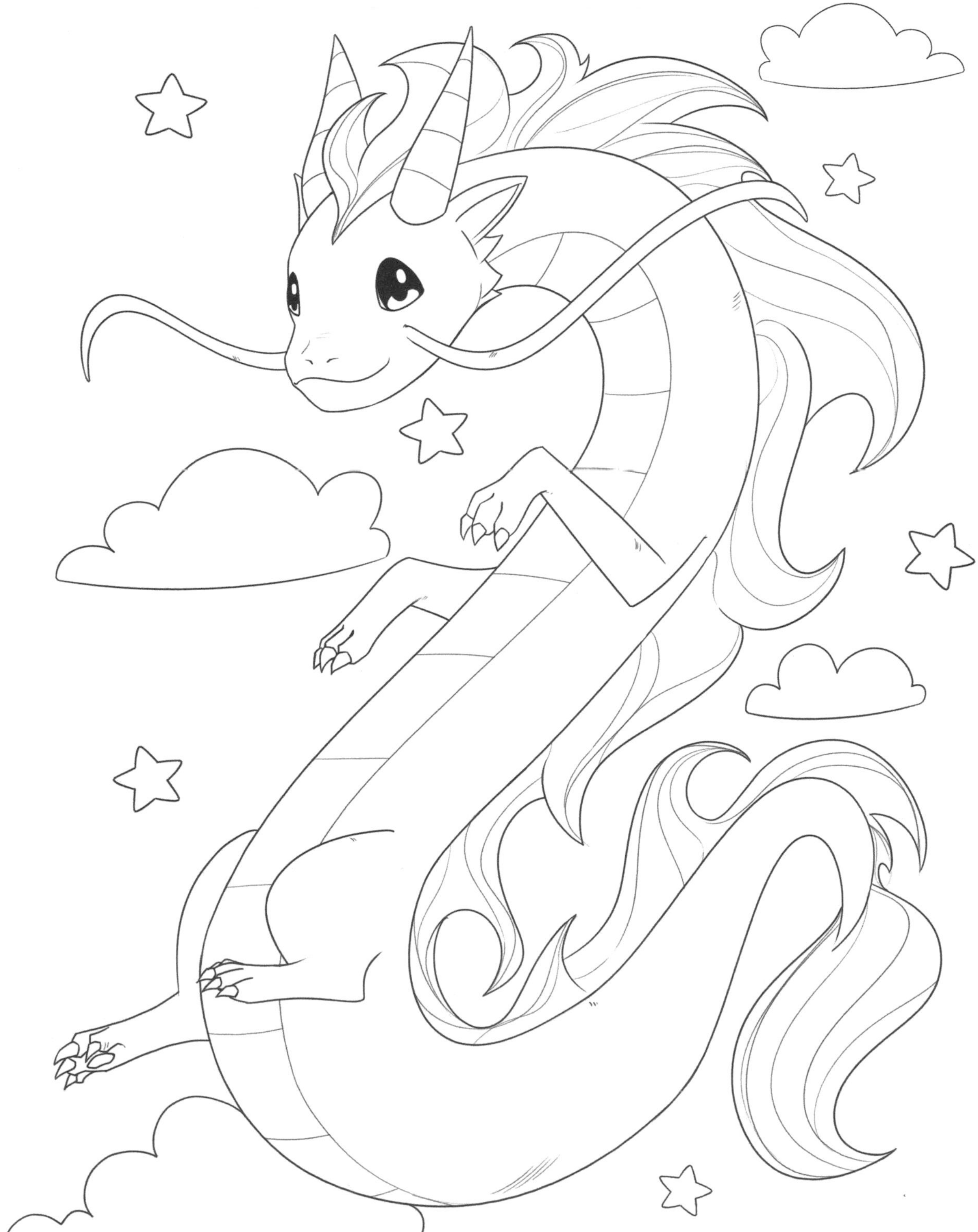

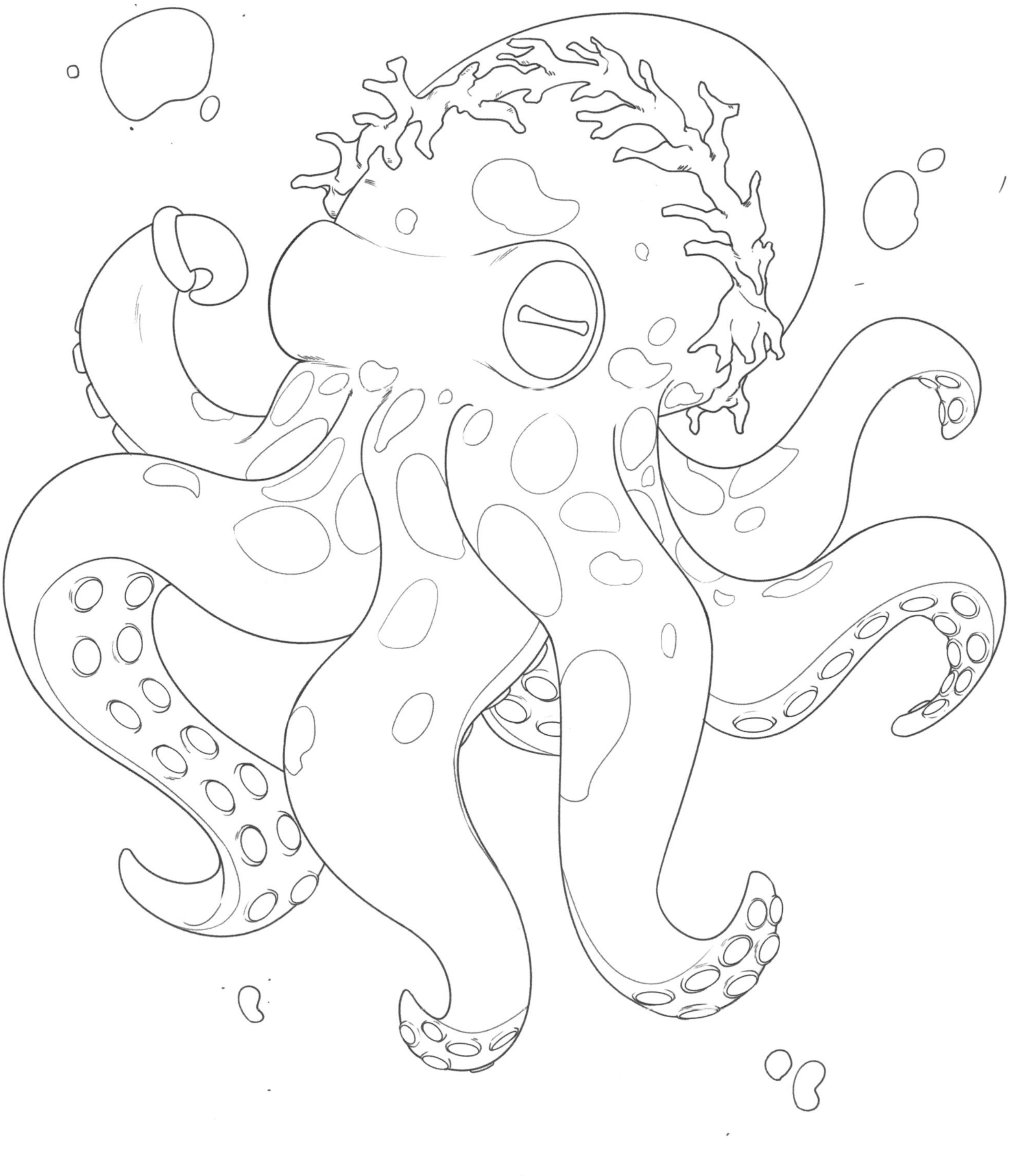

MAGICAL MANTRA FOR
FINDING LOVE AFTER FIGHTING CRIME

With the right partner, love can be a healing salve. With the wrong partner, it can become a draining daily battle. Healthy love is birthed from self-acknowledgment and -acceptance. The more we accept our own flaws as well as our partner's, work to defeat our own inner monsters, and create firm boundaries for ourselves and others, the more chances we have to cultivate true love. Save the fighting and strife for the battlefield. Love should fill every nook, cranny, and crevice of your safe spaces with a warming light and joy.

Repeat this:

I deserve a love that adds joy to my life.

MAGICAL MANTRA FOR
ACCEPTING BOUNDARIES

Boundaries create doors to our sacred, safe spaces. They're a reflection of how well we know, respect, and love ourselves. As you should set boundaries that keep your door open only to those you're comfortable with, you should also respect the boundaries set by others.

Yes, it can hurt to feel you've been "denied access," but a shut door doesn't signify defeat. It's a gift and a sign that that space wouldn't be a comfortable place for either party at that moment. If you've reached for the knob only to feel the door's been locked shut, remember the boundary and move on.

Repeat this:

A boundary is not an attack. I will accept and respect the boundaries of others and take them as a sign of love and respect.

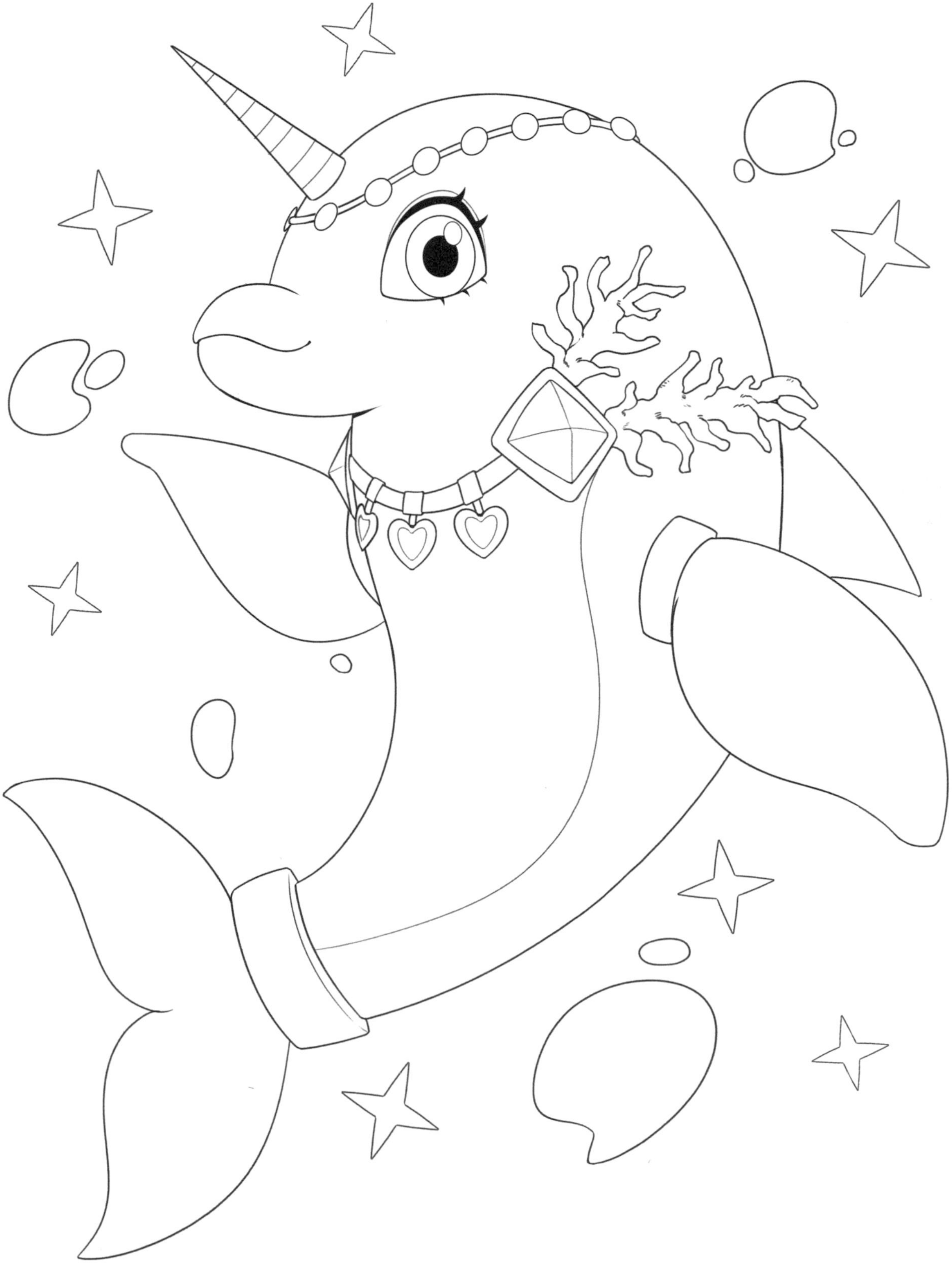

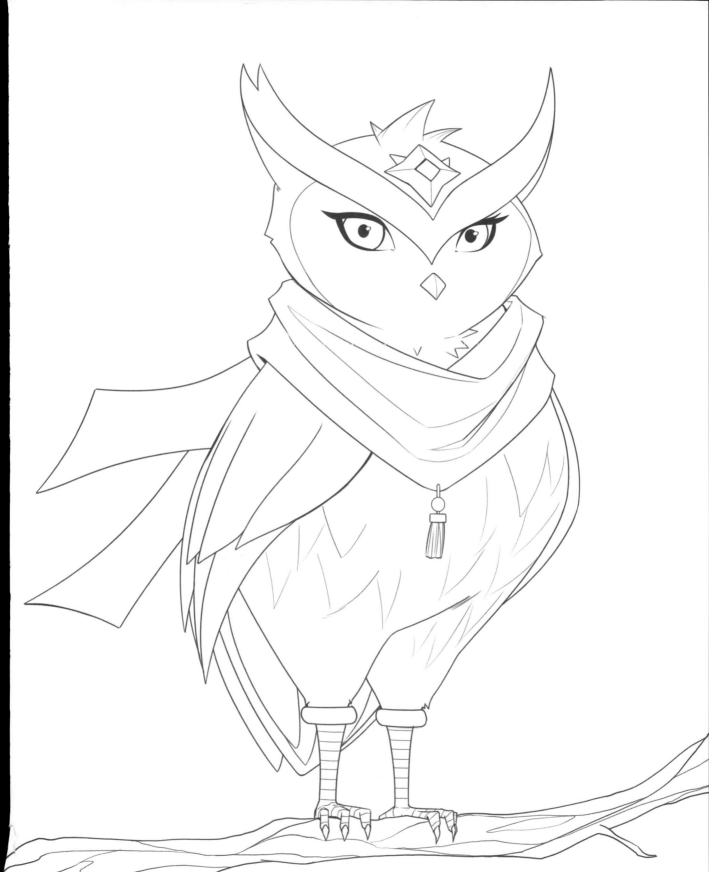

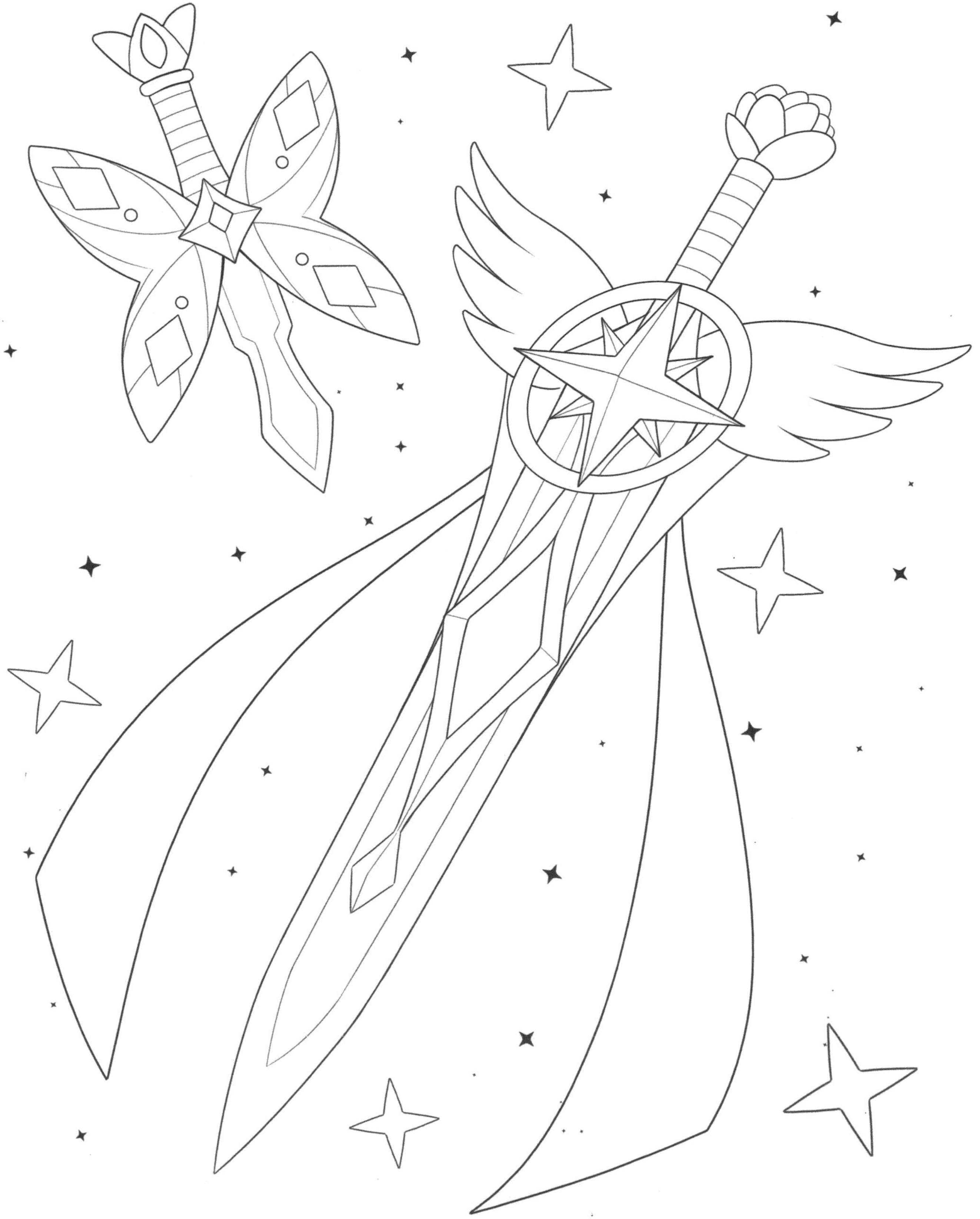

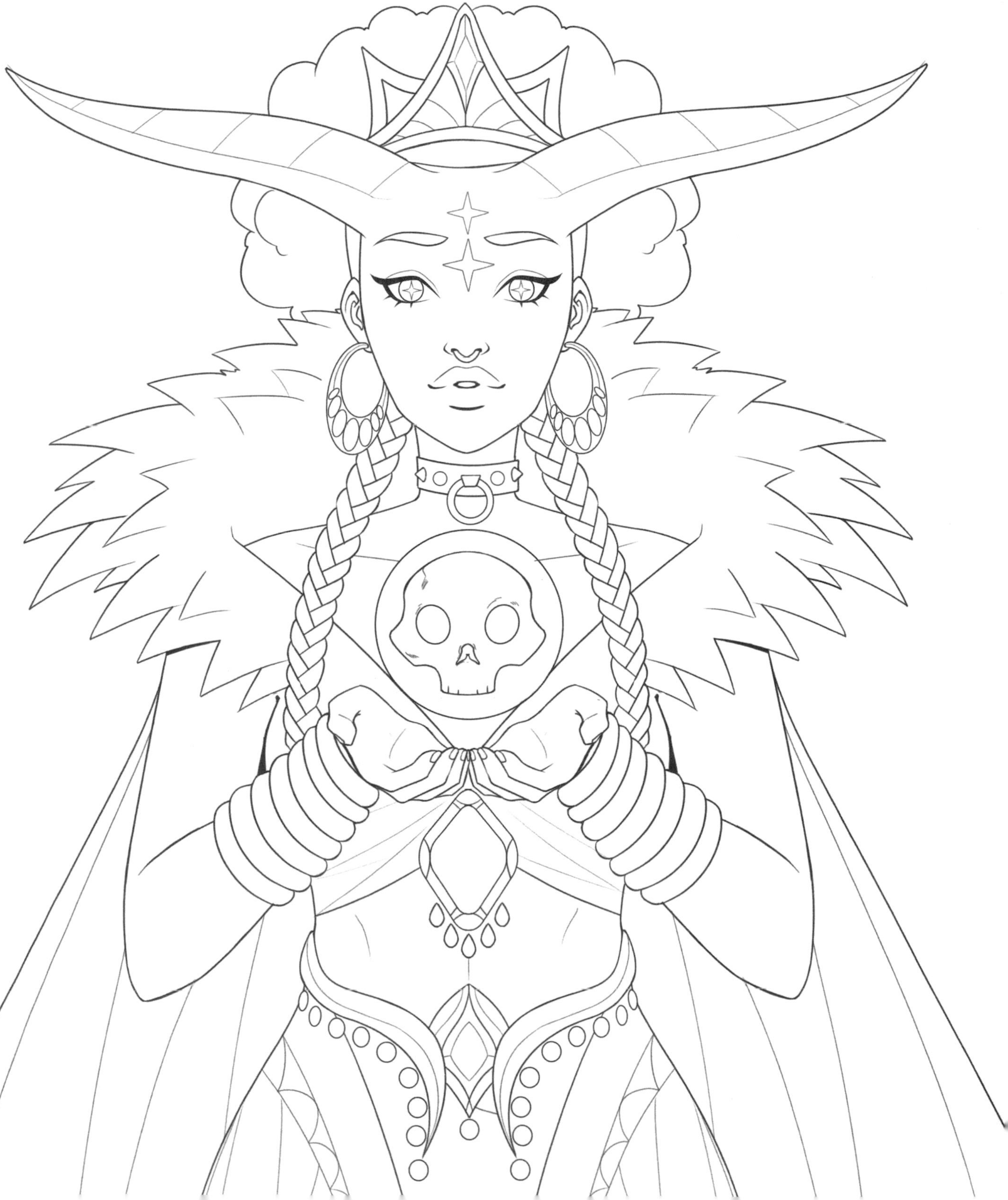

MAGICAL MANTRA FOR
FREEING YOURSELF FROM EXPECTATIONS

Carrying the weight of the world's expectations can create chaos within you and tamper with your magical energy and self-esteem. Do what your heart desires. Make moves that move you.

Repeat this:

I can create a life that I love. I'm not chained to anyone's expectations of how my life should look.

MAGICAL MANTRA FOR
OVERCOMING IMPOSTOR SYNDROME

Hey, magical girl. Don't listen to that inner voice that whispers that you don't belong. You work hard, and you belong in every room you find yourself in—no matter what anyone says!

Repeat this:

I belong in every room I find myself in.

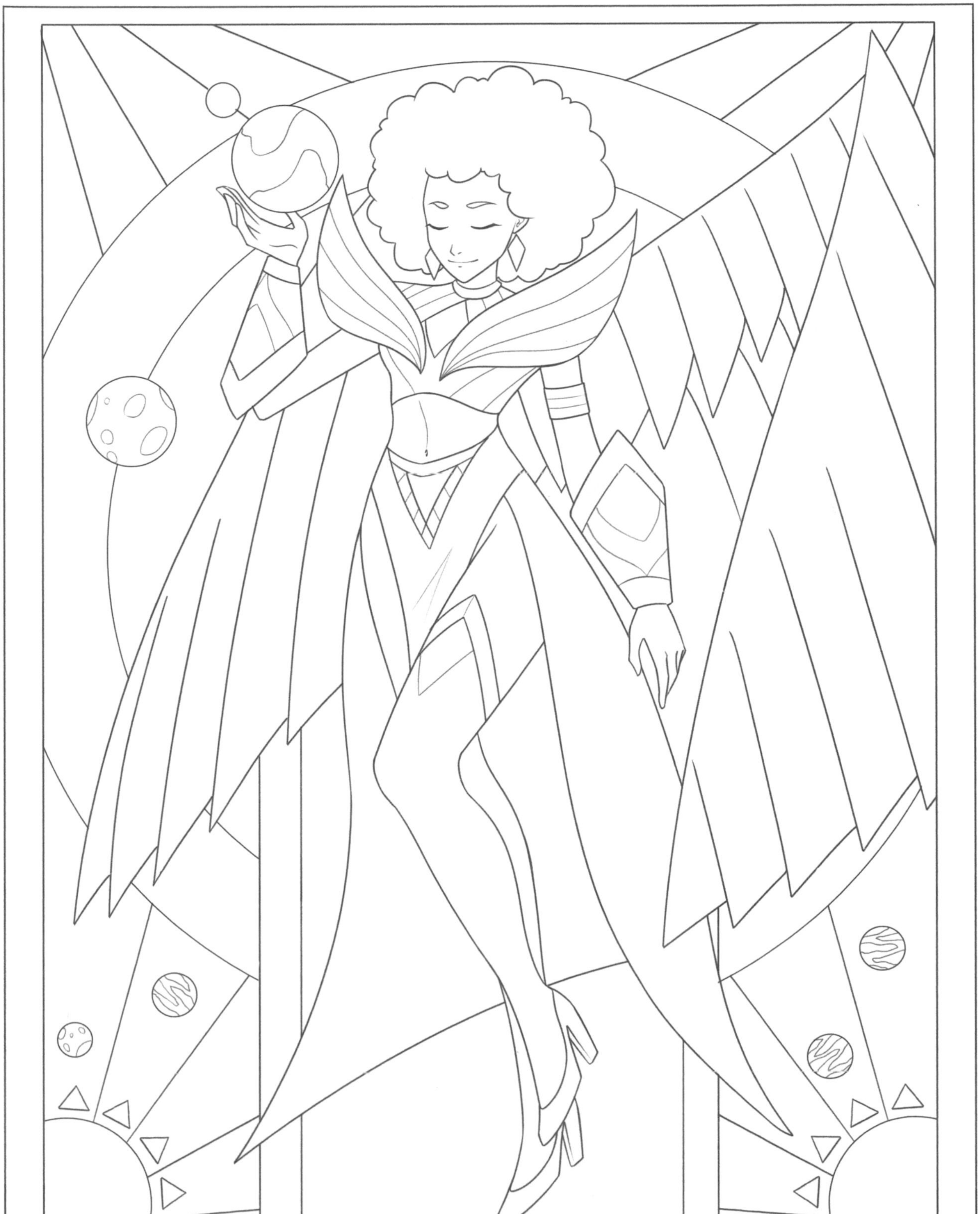

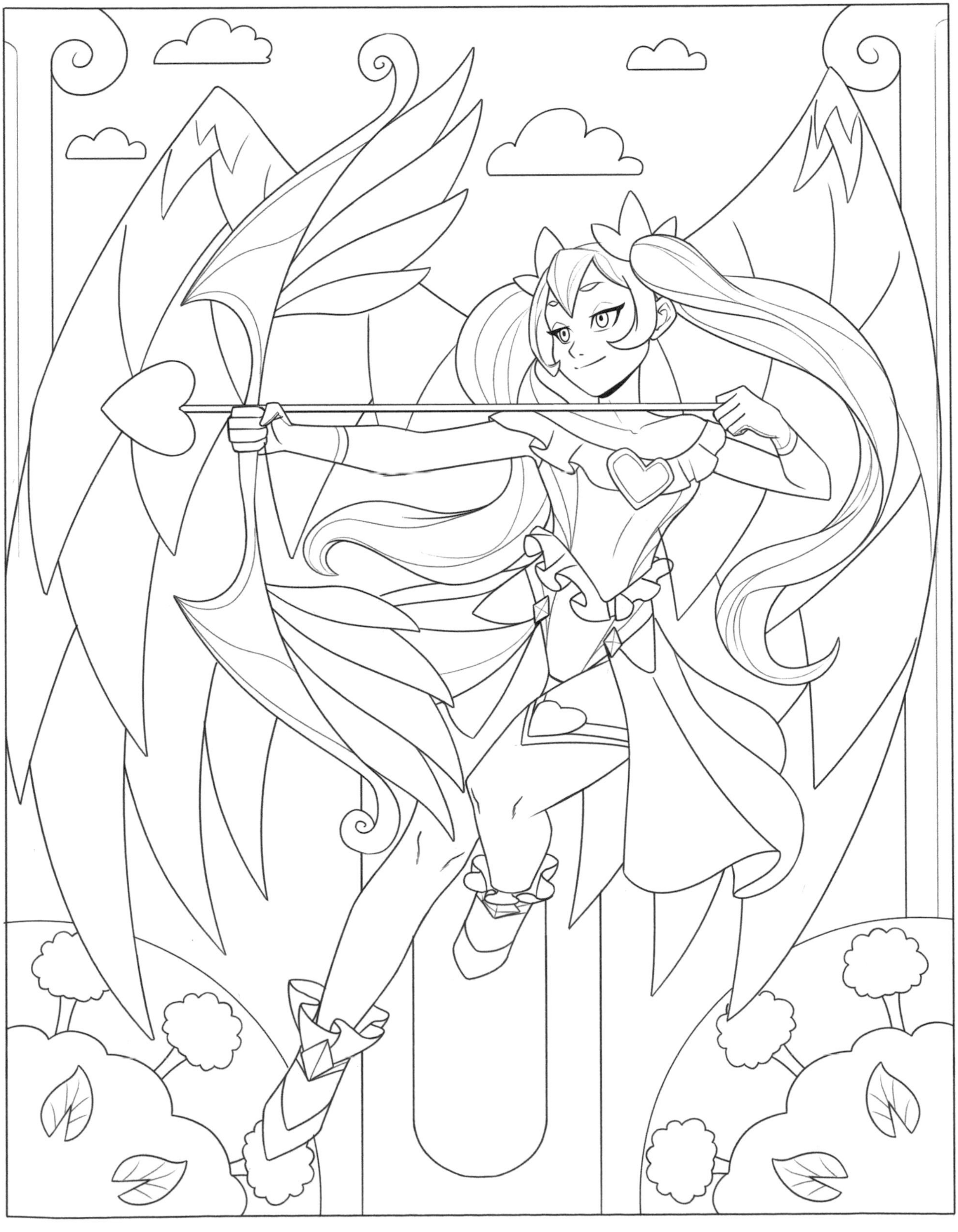

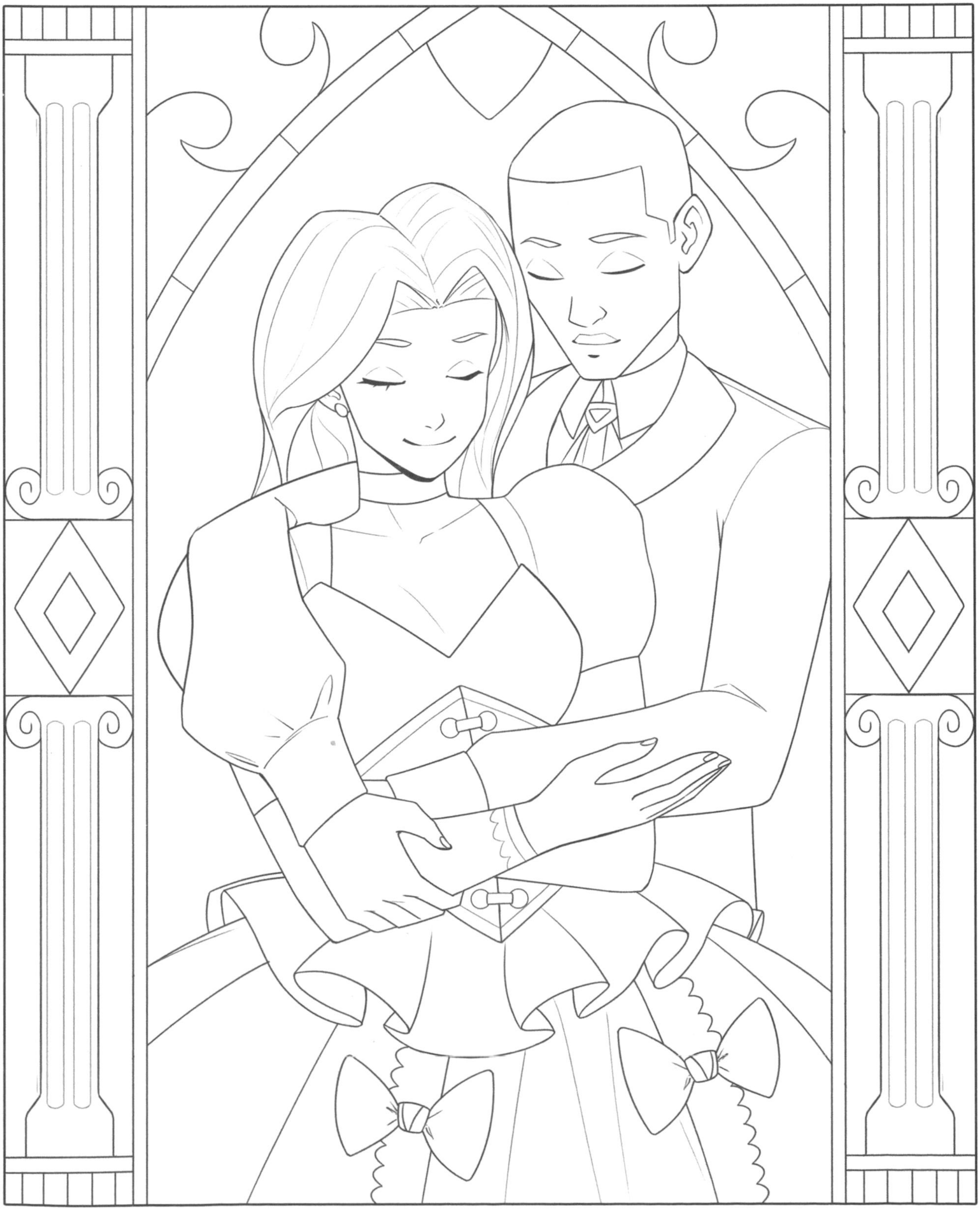

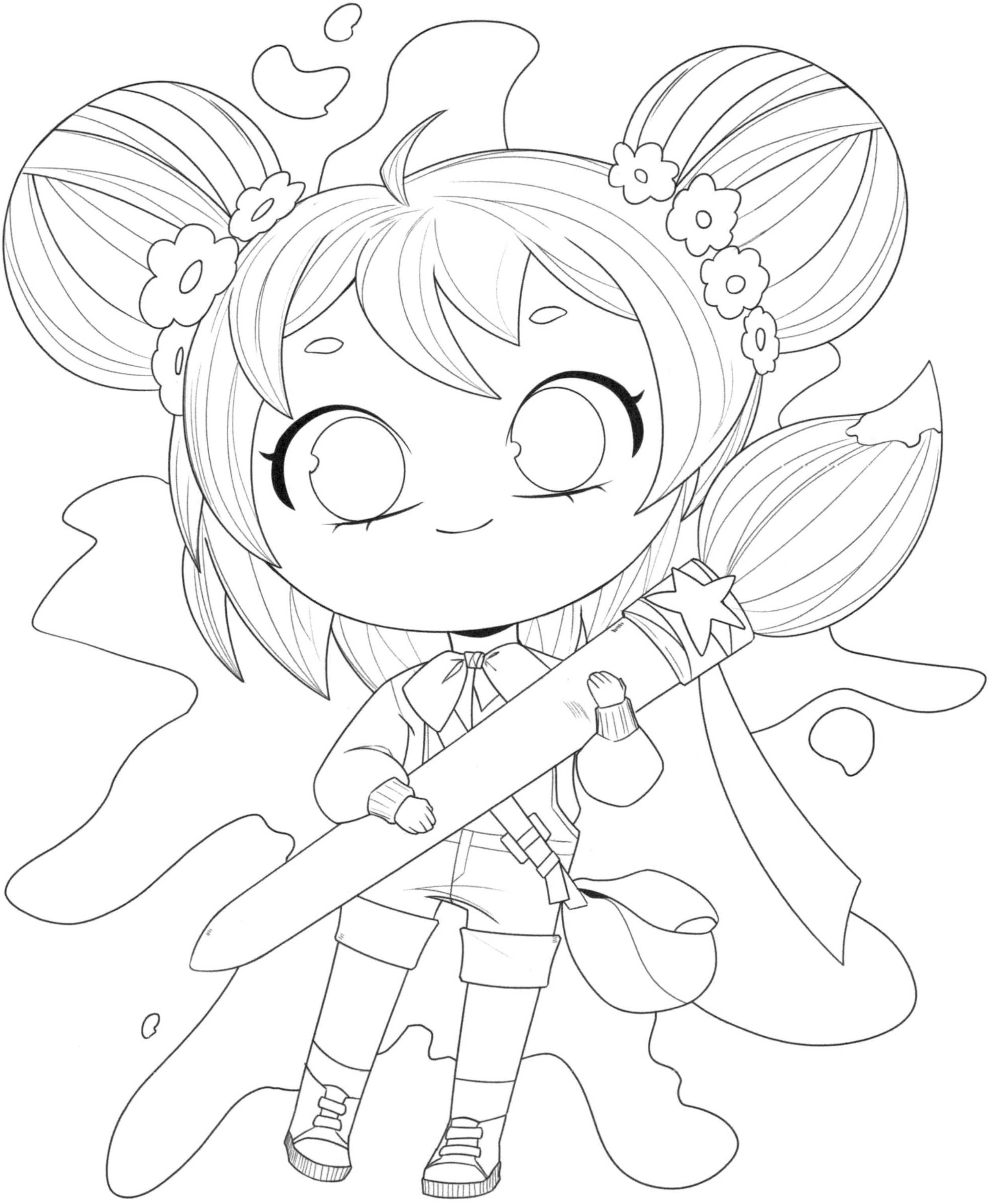

MAGICAL MANTRA FOR
KNOWING YOU'RE MORE THAN YOUR CAREER

You're on this planet to be your full, magical self, separate from what you do or have done for work. You're much more than your career. You're the laughter you share, the shoulder you offer your friends to cry on. You're the hugs you give, the impact you leave on your tiny world. Securing a job is an amazing accomplishment, but it doesn't define you.

Repeat this:

I am much more than my career.

MAGICAL MANTRA FOR
LISTENING TO YOUR INTUITION

That inner feeling you have, like a string tugging you along in a destined direction, is your intuition. Your intuition sends signals through your body when you're in danger, makes you feel warm and fuzzy when you're safe and loved, and knows your deepest desires. Don't let the noise from the outside world, or even that pesky inner voice of anxiety, stop you from being in tune with your intuition. Trust yourself.

Repeat this:

I will trust my intuition and go where I feel safe.

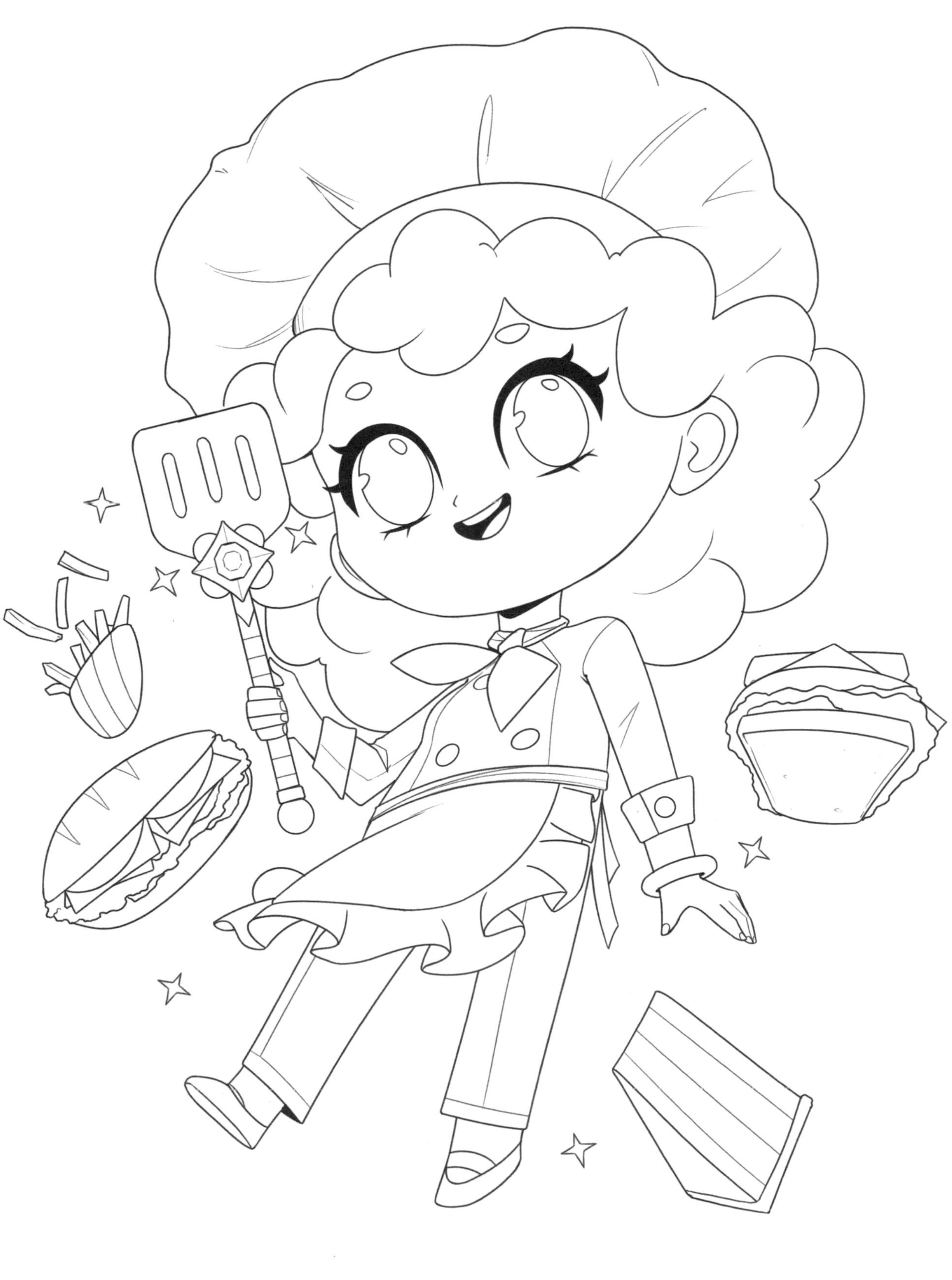

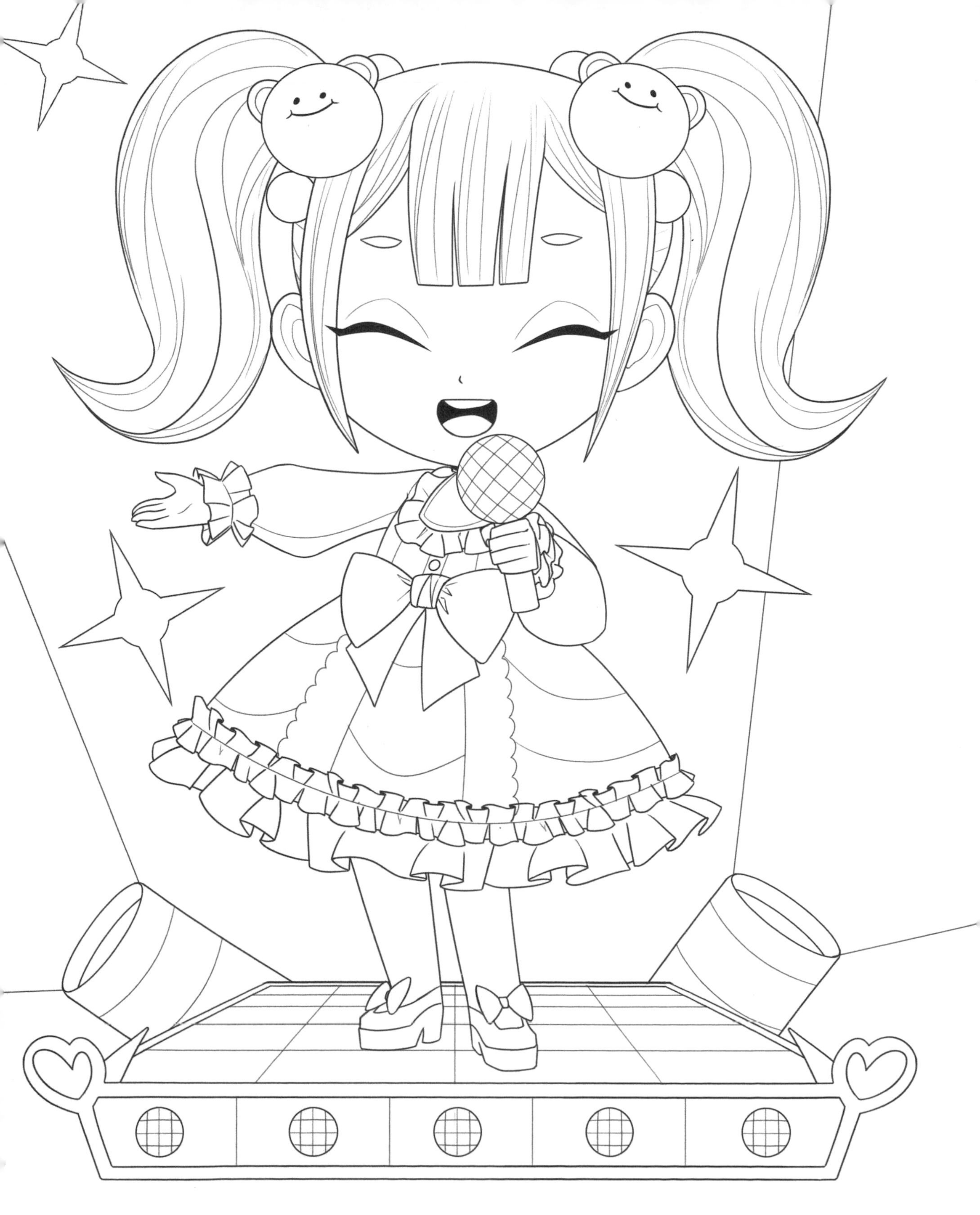

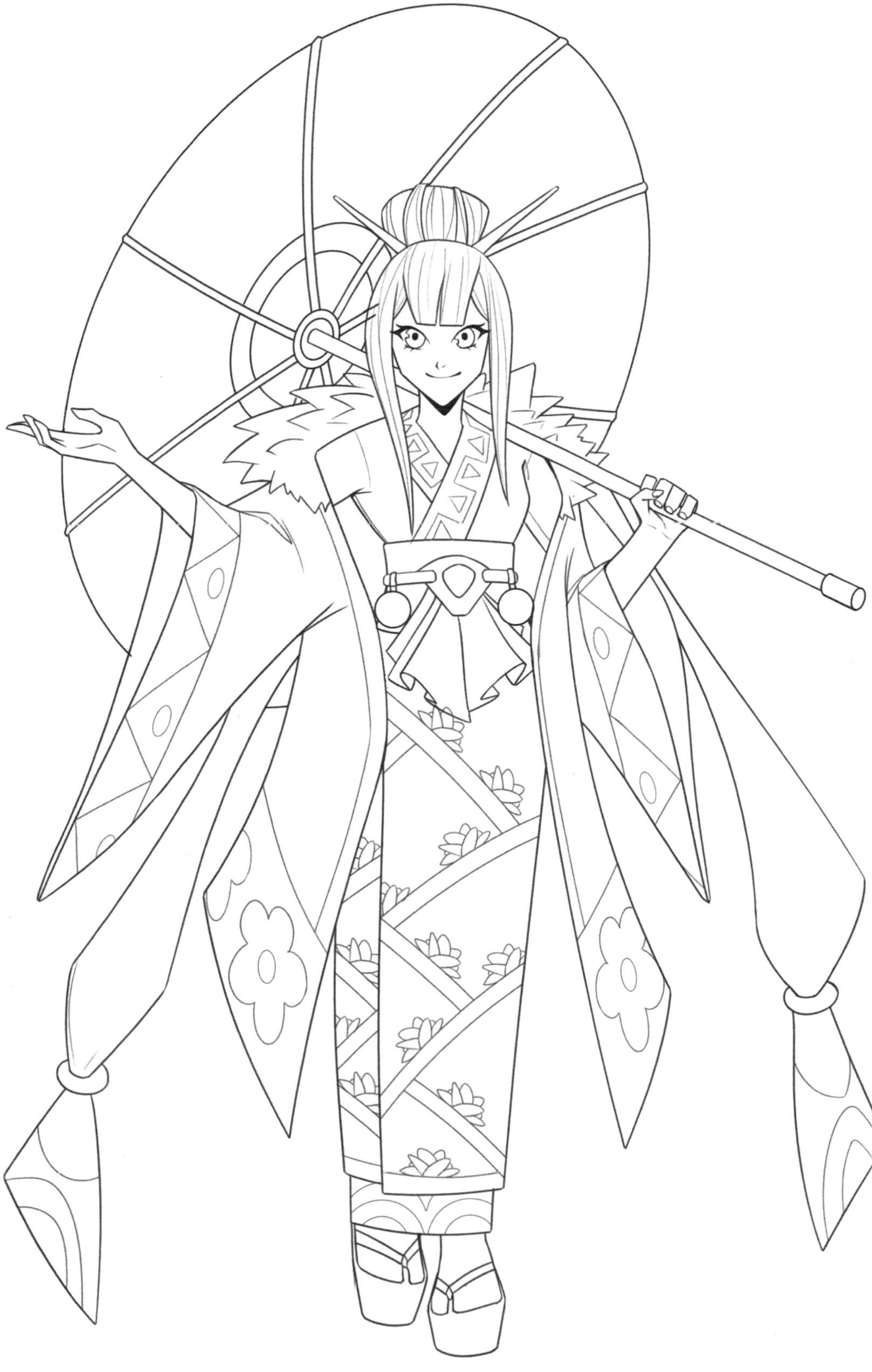

MAGICAL MANTRA FOR
ANXIETY

Your Anxiety Monster is lying to you. You're not less capable or knowledgeable than the next person. Stumbling over your words isn't the end of the world. Most people are so invested in their own lives that they aren't giving too much thought to yours. The next time that Anxiety Monster makes your voice shake or your eyes well up with tears, remember its words aren't reality. Keep showing up.

Repeat this:

I won't believe my Anxiety Monster's lies.

MAGICAL MANTRA FOR
HEALING

Never feel bad for continuing to feel, even when others don't understand. We can't control our emotions, and grief and heartbreak have no set timeline. The world tells us to "move on," even when our hearts still hurt. Heal in ways that work for you. There's no shame in healing at your own pace.

Repeat this:
I won't feel bad for feeling my emotions.

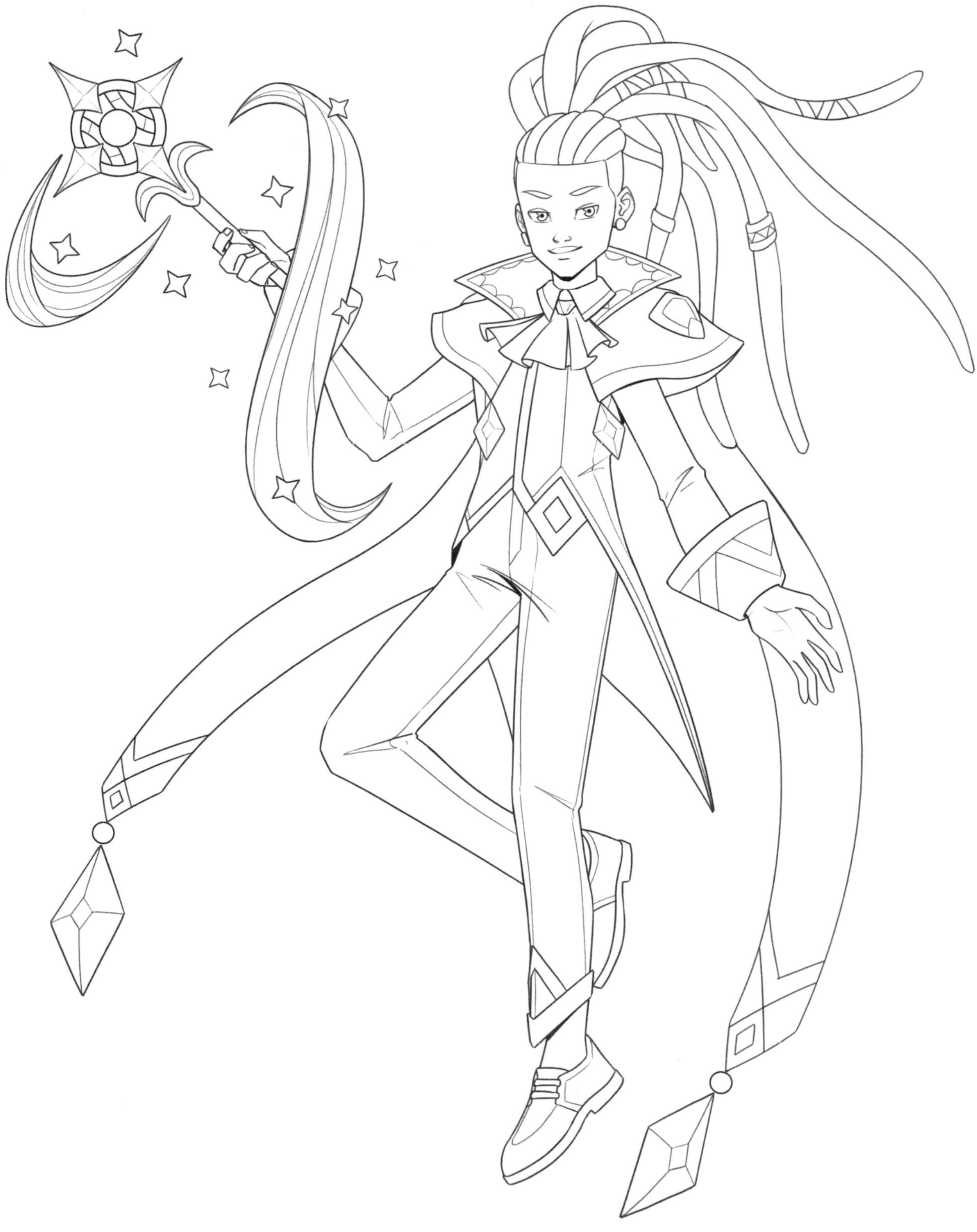

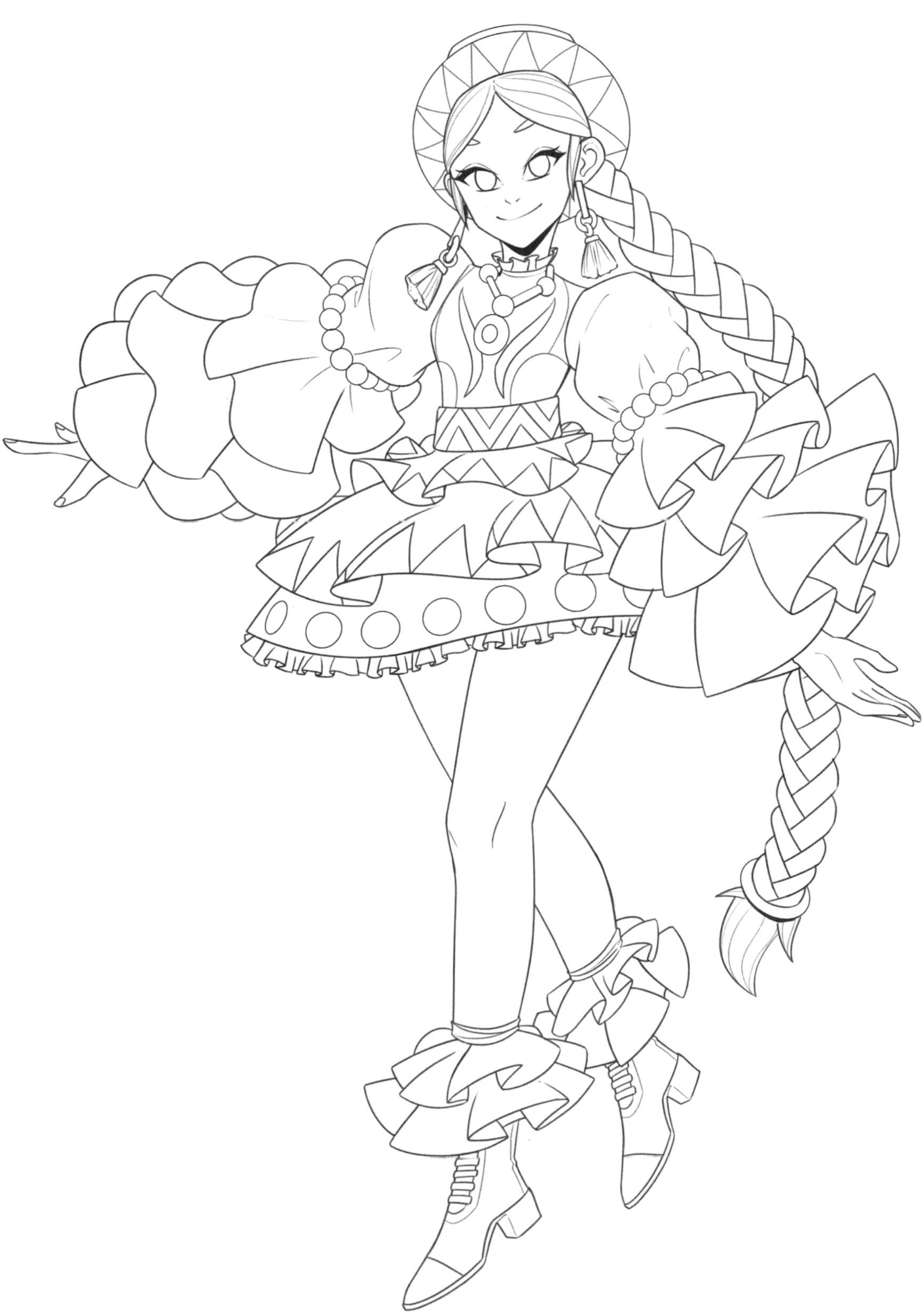

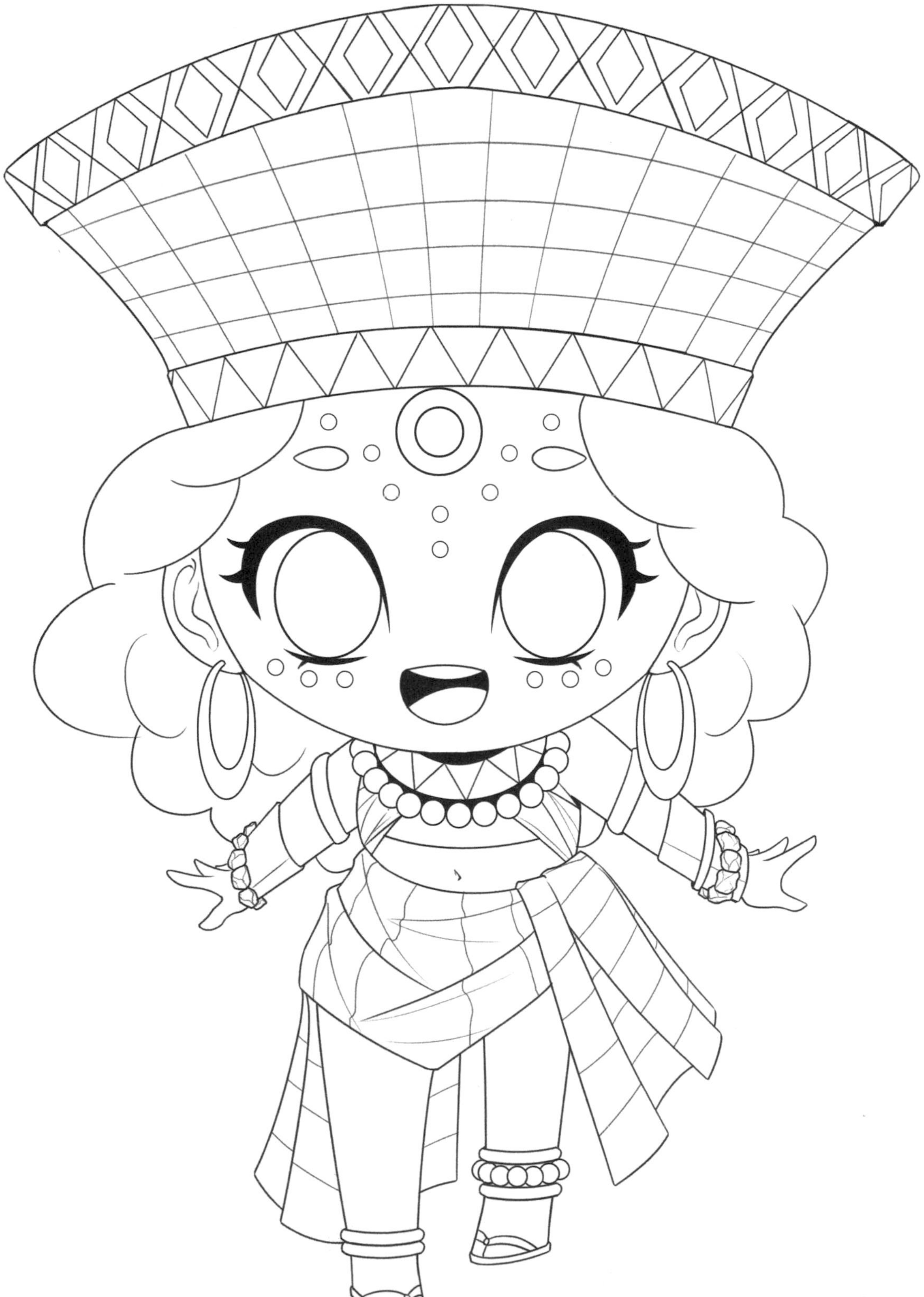

MAGICAL MANTRA FOR
FRIENDSHIP BREAKUPS

All relationships have a beginning and an end. The "when" depends on many factors—time, space, and changing boundaries can all contribute to the death of a friendship. It hurts when you can't reach out to someone you were once close to. Or when you silently and slowly drift apart. But it's part of life. Learn the lesson, if there is one, and continue on your journey. Who knows what other magical connections you'll make along the way?

Repeat this:

I appreciate the time I spent with friends in the past, and my heart is still open to new connections.

OUTRO

I'm so proud of you, magical girl! You've colored your world, defeated your monsters, and saved the day with self-care. If you want more magical, battle-ready tips, read *The Magical Girl's Guide to Life*! Or listen to *The Magical Girl's Guide to Life* podcast, where we discuss everything from mental health to magical girls to finding love after fighting crime.

Stay magical, and remember to rest!